What happened to
AMERICA'S
Middle Class?

Why is this wealthy class in Decline?
How to Avoid Being Left Behind

RICO VIDAS

WESTBOW
PRESS®
A DIVISION OF THOMAS NELSON
& ZONDERVAN

WestBow Press books may be ordered through booksellers or by contacting:

WestBow Press
A Division of Thomas Nelson & Zondervan
1663 Liberty Drive
Bloomington, IN 47403
www.westbowpress.com
844-714-3454

ISBN: 978-1-6642-8689-4 (sc)
ISBN: 978-1-6642-8688-7 (hc)
ISBN: 978-1-9736-9969-9 (e)

Library of Congress Control Number: 2023909854

Print information available on the last page.

WestBow Press rev. date: 06/21/2023

Contents

Introduction

Why I Wrote This Book

There was a time when, as a young man who had been licensed to practice law, I realized that despite my supposedly superior education, I saw only limitations to my knowledge and experience. For my age, I had considerable practical political education through experiences I would continue to build, but not with the intention of becoming a full-time politician. I wanted power so that I, and my family, would not be pawns to other powerful men who couldn't care less about our well-being.

At age nineteen, through the good office of a congressman, I had received an appointment from my political hero, President John F. Kennedy, to the labor department in Washington, DC. Once there, I was released to work as an intern in the offices of Congressman George E. Brown Jr. It was the summer of 1963, the year Dr. Martin Luther King Jr. gave his "I Have a Dream" speech and President Kennedy was assassinated. It was a heady experience for a nineteen-year-old biracial Mexican American refugee of the gang wars in East Los Angeles. Before I followed some of my friends into the cemetery, my mother's income enabled a move to the suburbs. I received an excellent education in a White suburban high school district that had initiated an accelerated honors program as a response to the launch of Sputnik, the world's first satellite placed in orbit by our communist rival, the Soviet Union. I saw an opportunity to overcome my ignorance and ineptness and, at the urging of two of my teachers, applied for entry. My desire and effort were recognized by my teachers who secured for me, over multiple objections, that all-important opportunity to participate and earn my way. They gave me a chance, and generally that is all I ever needed. I went from a failing student to straight As, student body president, and a football scholarship to a small liberal arts college.

I started working in political campaigns, earned my way, and ended up in Washington, DC. I went by Greyhound Bus and returned to Los Angeles by jet airplane. It mirrored my growth. When I came back, I decided that I never wanted to return to Washington, DC, unless it was in one of two capacities: US senator or fat cat who controlled senators with sizable campaign contributions and had the influence that showed it. Of the two, I preferred fat cat.

It was then I realized that there were financial forces at work that had influences on which the public was not privy. I wondered whether this was healthy for a democracy. As one of my labor friends described it, "This ain't no democracy. It's a ... moneyocracy!" And our side did not have the money, except for some exceptions like the Kennedys who ended up assassinated. JFK's murder made me realize that those invisible forces not only had money, but they also had anonymity with which to exert their power. Now fifty years later, I believe that both FBI Director J. Edgar Hoover and Vice President Lyndon Johnson were involved in the assassination, but they were only tools of other powerful forces who had a vested interest different from my own.

It was not lost on me that Kennedy, in October 1963, had ordered all American military forces out of Vietnam. Then, after Kennedy was assassinated on November 22, 1963, Vice President Lyndon Johnson became president and one of his first actions was countermanding that order, which seemed to foretell that there would be a much bigger war that my generation would have to fight. If John Kennedy did not think it was necessary, why should I believe a war in Vietnam was necessary?

It was then that I decided to embark on a study of what I referred to as a study of the technology of money. I really wanted to find the fundamental sources of power for which money was only a symptom. I knew that those who exerted such anonymous power had no intention of ever exposing their identities or allowing themselves to undergo scrutiny.

As a young man, I harbored illusions of becoming sufficiently wealthy to earn my way into the club. I now know that although I may have become an occasional guest, my pedigree and background doomed any thought of ever being considered an equal, no matter how rich I became. I believe this was the experience that Joseph P. Kennedy, the patriarch of the Kennedy family and the creator of their wealth, had encountered for being Irish. But that was not my goal.

My goal is to protect my extended family and my complicated, diverse, and extended diasporas including all disadvantaged poor children of any race who also want to better themselves and do good works for humankind.

At the time, I decided that I would go as far as possible in making money and looking for the sources of anonymous power. I would then write down what I learned so that those who came after me would have my experiences to build on and learn from. I did not expect to complete the journey but would chronicle my progress and hand it on to those who would come after me.

Instead, I believe I have found success not where I thought it would be but as a by-product of the effort. This book explains my discoveries, analysis, and conclusions along with a call to action to become free economically and have the capability of living in a true democracy.

My analysis indicates that I don't have to know the identity of my adversaries so long as I can see the symptoms of their power and defend against them. The fundamental element of their power is money. Their minions are politicians, lawyers, and bankers. That tells me that I must play offense and defense. I need to have the support and control of serious money and like-minded politicians, lawyers, and bankers to play defense to protect our joint, and several, vested interests. Our defense is to assemble the people, money, and other resources to effectively play defense in their game.

Then our offense begins with entering a different arena where their money and power are irrelevant to our goals, power, and operations. We play a totally different game where there is no opening or motivations for them. They are irrelevant to what we do. Money is not key to our game. We can operate without money. But we can command all the goods and services money can buy. They have money and anonymity, we have money and irrelevance to begin with, and we will develop anonymity for our vested interests as time passes. We will use the capabilities we develop to defend our interests.

We analyze two issues to our plan. To let the story unfold, we follow two narratives. Part 1 is the current arena of money and leverage. Part 2 is the new economic model we will create to initiate a new era of economic democracy.

The story will unfold in these two parts:

- Part 1: Financial Leverage
- Part 2: "Lessons of Nature" Using Virus Tactics for Finance

There appear to be these two well-defined paths toward major financial success in America, and they are evaluated in part 2 of this treatise:

- Path 1: Banking and Leverage
- Path 2: An Alternative I Refer to as the Five Elements Solution

Concepts and Maxims of Political Power

To understand much that I will relate in this book, background on the nature of political power will help build a matrix that will enable the reader to gain an accurate understanding of my message. The following concepts and maxims are intended to lay a foundation for understanding the reasoning and operations of political power:

- **The Iron Law of Oligarchy.**

  Robert Michaels's sociological study of nineteenth-century Italian labor unions forcefully develops his contention that power quickly comes to reside with a small group at the top of the power pyramid. They get into a position to call the shots and manipulate power moves within their society. They may be called by any name, such as the Mafia heads of families, the board of directors, the kitchen cabinet, the executive caucus, or the trade association. They will rule until some upstart gains, generally after escaping attempts to assassinate the leaders, sufficient power to successfully challenge them. They will then generally expand to bring in and either adjust to or co-opt the upstart. Always look to a small group, generally speaking through a spokesman and composed of anonymous powerful members, at the top calling the shots and manipulating events, to figure out what is going on. Follow the money and wealth to see who benefits from the events to point you in the right direction.

- **The Iron Law of Vested Interest**

  When I was in college, I used to engage in pseudointellectual discussions of sophomore ideas on politics, the economy, justice, religion, the nature of education, and all topics on which we had opinions. We thought, using logic, we could convince our friends and associates to adopt our stances as correct.

The great flaw in intellectual discourse and debate is an underlying mistaken assumption that men are reasonable, will follow logic, and do what is appropriately indicated. John Herman Randall states, "Man is a rational animal, but his animality is more deeply rooted than his rationality. He cannot live by Truth alone." What is true will not determine the actions men will take or the outcome.

Ben Franklin said, "If you would persuade, speak of interest, not of reason."

He is right; vested interest determines the actions that men will agree to, not truth. It is nice if truth is included in the mixture as part of the persuasive oratory for those who, like engineers and scientists, must depend on and believe in the superiority of truth, but it is not necessary to action. In the actions of men, vested interest will always prevail. The task of the righteous is to bring about a convergence of vested interest and truth so that truth is the primary vested interest to be protected.

- **There Are No Eternal Enemies or Eternal Friends, Only Eternal Interests**

This is a quote from a speech by President John Kennedy concerning politics among nations.

- **Power Determines Politics among Nations**

This is clearly seen when viewing the conduct of nation-states, but it is less clear elsewhere. Corporations are today's shadow nations, and the superrich determine their real vested interest.

When I was a youth, I found myself in a White Republican stronghold. I was born a Democrat and, as taught by my parents, a proud member of a minority. Some of the educators and pastors in the suburb to which my mother had moved and purchased a home taught me that corporations had to be good stewards of the public's interest and were the protectors of democracy. It is always election time for corporations, and you vote for them with paying dollars for goods and services that the public wants and needs. The corporation determines what the public needs and wants (the market) and finds a way to provide it at a price that will maintain customer support. If a competitor can do it better and cheaper, then they will get the support in the form of dollars paid for the goods and services provided. It is in the interest of the corporations to be good stewards of the public's welfare. This same argument can be made for the nation-states of the world.

But do corporations see it that way? Are they public servants or amoral tools of profit and control to satisfy the immediate needs of the myopic and the greedy? In the 1950s and 1960s, the major constituents of American society, the lower, working, middle, and upper classes, had been forced into an informal partnership by a common enemy during World War II. After the war, they continued to work together for the common good and built the world's greatest economy. This is where the modern middle class emerged as, up to that time, the wealthiest class to have ever existed in the history of the planet. However, that partnership began to fall apart with the divergence of interest put into clear focus by the war in Vietnam. Middle-class children were being sent to die in a trumped-up war from which the military-industrial complex was profiting enormously. It is here that we begin to witness the true nature of modern American corporate and upper class greed. Its fangs, greed, and ruthlessness became visible to the middle class. The middle class rebelled against the war using student protest as its shock troops and the ballot box as its long-term strategy.

Since that time, the middle class has been under attack but doesn't seem to know it. This topic will be explored in later sections of this book, but right now it is only too necessary to survey the fruits of corporate greed as it affected the middle class.

Big tobacco corporations claimed for years that their products did not cause cancer, and their products, with the full knowledge and acquiescence of the corporations' major owners, proceeded to kill millions of Americans while operating in broad daylight.

The PBS documentary *The Power of Big Oil* shows how with full knowledge of the consequences, the oil industry chose to preserve immediate profits and allow it products to savage the planet with global warming. We have seen chemical companies do great harm to an ignorant public.

Rather than being good servants of the public interest, the message from some of America's largest and most profitable corporations, and the wealthy owners who control them, has been a clear lesson: the public's interest is not our concern. The law is clear that corporate officers have a fiduciary duty to their shareholders to maximize profit. As a result, they can and will hire smart public relations firms and spokesmen along with smart consultants to confuse and misinform a public that many times is not sufficiently sophisticated to see through the deceptions and misrepresentations. They will do all that is needed to preserve immediate profits. Others can worry about the long term.

- **Money Is the Mother's Milk of Politics**

Power is effective at all levels but must be fueled by money.

- **Money, Power, and Ruthlessness**

I was inspired watching the presidential debates in 1960 between John Kennedy and Richard Nixon. I volunteered to work in a local congressional campaign, and not long after, a local congressman hired me to work in his campaign organization. I joined the Young Democrats at Whittier College, Republican Richard Nixon's alma mater. I then spent the next two years immersed in partisan politics, power struggles at endorsing conventions, paper wars tearing down the opposition's signs and putting up our own with wallpaper glue, canvasing voters door to door, and preparing mass mailing campaigns. What I discovered was that treachery was everywhere. Allies would turn out to be spies working for the other side. People would promise to vote for your side, then switch at the last minute. Initially, it was hard to spot betrayers. With experience, however, it got easier to spots the liars. Sometimes, when their votes were critical, political power would be employed to pressure them into voting the right way. These could be vicious.

When the stakes were high, it became expected that everyone would involve ruthless tactics. "We are not playing around here. You must understand that this is serious business and there is no room for weak sisters!" People would be threatened, fired from their jobs, cut off from opportunities, and have any vulnerability that could be exposed attacked. With experience, one finds that the ruthlessness comes with the territory. Ruthlessness is a feature of dealing with power and competition when the stakes are high. I have seen it in politics. But I have also seen it in business competition and in lawsuits. Betrayal is a fact of life, and forgiveness is a sign of weakness and not to be tolerated. Those who can't be ruthless when necessary generally will not last long. They will be outmaneuvered, not able to muster resources, and be outvoted by candidates with more financial backing and the support of other ruthless politicians who know how to consolidate power.

• James the Just versus Cesare Borgia

How can nations commit war crimes and corporations engage in activity (tobacco poison and oil global warming) that end up killing people, even though indirectly? Politics among nations are governed by power. To understand how such cruelty can become business as usual among supposedly civilized people, one must understand the difference between personal morality and public morality. We will explore this phenomenon by examining three versions of the golden rule: the Christian golden rule, the business golden rule, and the banker's golden rule.

First to understand the concept of public versus personal morality, we will review the experiences of James the Just and Cesare Borgia. Both were princes ruling over city-states in Italy during the Renaissance. James ruled a city-state as a benevolent leader, attempting to be fair and just in all his decisions. He was considered a very good man and devout practicing Christian. One day an enemy showed up at the entrance to his city and demanded his surrender. He refused to surrender and requested that his advisors come up with a plan. They did, but it was a deception that required him to lie. He said that his personal morality would not permit him to bear false witness and lie. The enemy attacked and easily conquered the city, killed all the men, and sold the women and children into slavery. Cesare Borgia found himself in a similar situation, but when it came time to lie, he did not hesitate to lie with apparent integrity and did what was necessary to enable his forces to defeat the enemy. He saved his city-state from the enemy.

James the Just was a very good man but a very bad prince. James's morality was ideal for a civilized Christian society. The people looking to him for protection were of less importance to him than his higher personal moral imperative. In contrast, Cesare Borgia was a terrible person but a very good prince. Public morality was his priority. The Christian golden rule is an appropriate guide for civilize men governed pursuant to the rule of law in a civilized land.

When a hostile military force shows up at your gate, concepts of personal morality become irrelevant. The rule of law in a civilized land becomes irrelevant. The business golden rule is now relevant. Do unto others before they do it to you. The reason is that the ruling law is now kill or be killed, the law of the jungle. It is survival of the fittest. If you follow the Christian golden rule, you will soon be somebody's meal.

In the arena of competition for food for survival, for great wealth, or great empire, ruthlessness will set in, and the jungle will provide the governing law. Kill or be killed, but kill off the competition before they kill you. The opposition can be competitors, agents of the government, or vigilante do-gooders. The most effective tend to be competitors. They are after the same money and power that you have, want, or covet. Money and power can be used to neutralize the government. If vigilantes do something illegal, they can be killed off. It is the competitors who can, and will, engage in prolonged warfare fighting the battle for survival of the fittest who will test your mettle.

So the Christian golden rule is appropriate for a civilized society, but if confronted with fierce competition, it is the business golden rule that is appropriate. However, the most insidious and dangerous is the third: the banker's golden rule. "He who has the gold makes the rules." The problem bankers present is that they work for the superrich. Because of their enormous power, they believe they can create and enforce any rule and make it stick. They dictate negotiating terms while financing business dealings and they seem to believe they are above the law.

Of the three rules, the banker's is the most dangerous because their masters are the superrich. Soon they believe that they can buy the right lawyers who can manipulate the law so that it doesn't touch them. They also, because of past successes, believe that they can force acceptance of the biggest of lies, especially when dealing with the government. Among their efforts that succeeded to some extent for extended periods are the following lies: "There is no such thing as global warming," "Tobacco is not addictive or a dangerous poison," and "The 2020 election was stolen."

Three golden rules are real. In a civilized society, the Christian golden rule is paramount. In a system where the law of the jungle and survival of the fittest prevail, it is the business golden rule that is paramount. But the group that controls all others are the superrich who control bankers. Their vested interest is narrow and can be hostile to America's middle class. That is just the way it is. So how can we change what negatively affects the middle class?

Change the place of money within our society! What happens when money has no value? In times of hyperinflation, coin, paper, digital cash, and bank accounts have little or no value. When the barter value of commodities is worth more than money, the power of money is replaced by barter power backed by possession of the commodities. Also, what happens if you create a substitute money that is backed by the commodities or other things of value that people will accept and that only people associated with you have?

If you lead a society that produces sufficient food to feed a nation, that power to produce the necessary goods and services required to survive implies that power has shifted and that society's masses who produce the essential commodities can control destinies. In this situation, your workers control society's necessities, and money is useless.

But money is very convenient and can be useful. The solution to which we should aspire is to produce life's necessities, then use them to secure sufficient money to be comfortable and secure. The fact that we produce life's necessities makes us independent. Because we avoid debt, we are free from creditors. We seek money for convenience rather than necessity. We are free to, but not compelled to, seek money for fun and profit. Furthermore, producing and selling life's necessary commodities can be a lucrative business. If money is the only game available, then bankers will always control. But there are alternatives.

- **Introduction of a New Order of Things**

It ought to be remembered that there is nothing more difficult to take in hand, more perilous to conduct, or more uncertain in its success, than to take the lead in the introduction of a new order of things. Because the innovator has for enemies all those who have done well under the old conditions, and lukewarm defenders in those who may do well under the new. This coolness arises partly from fear of the opponents, who have the laws on their side, and partly from the incredulity of men, who do not readily believe in new things until they have had a long experience of them. (Niccolò Machiavelli, *The Prince)*

- **Better to Be Loved or Feared**

Love is optional; fear is compelling. A prince should endeavor to be feared rather than loved but never be hated. Never take a man's property or his women. Men will sooner forgive the murder of their parents than the taking of their women or property.

- **If You Betray Me Once, When Pressed, You Will Betray Me Again**

If you hurt me once, it is your fault. If you hurt me twice (because I was forewarned and let you get into a position where you could do it again), it's my fault. So after betrayal, the logical political power response is to kill off the betrayer before he or she can cause irreparable damage. If the betrayer has close allies, then they also need to be killed off before they seek revenge. The Mafia understood this very well. Joseph Stalin took it to a pathological extreme and killed millions.

- **Patricians Who Take up the Cause of the Exploited Will Eventually Pay Dearly for Their Betrayal**

Rebellions that turn into successful revolutions have all been led by the middle class. This includes the four social revolutions that completely overturned the previous order: the French Revolution of 1789, the Mexican Revolution of 1910, the Russian Bolshevik Revolution of 1919, and the Chinese Communist Revolution of 1949.

Compare rebellions and revolutions to Plutarch's description using a serpent analogy where the body rose in rebellion to the head. The head's nature was to lead because it had eyes and could see, and the body did not. Leading was not in the body's nature; soon after it assumed leadership, it had caused such injury to itself going directly over sharp rocks that it could not move and bled profusely.

Patricians are privileged to receive the education and experience that allow them to see what the upper classes are doing, so that any who chose to do so may protect their lower-class constituents. But only at the risk of alienating the upper classes in inciting upper-class retaliations.

Many believe Franklin D. Roosevelt saved the upper class, of which he was a member, from a Marxist revolution during the Great Depression. He was hated by them for his good deed. The Roman brothers that Plutarch describes and the Kennedy brothers, John and Bobby, were assassinated for violating the vested interest of their class. For the Kennedys, they also violated both the vested interest of longtime FBI director J. Edgar Hoover and then Vice President Lyndon Johnson.

Lyndon Johnson as president delivered for Martin Luther King Jr. and the civil rights movement. Then King came out in opposition to Johnson's war in Vietnam. To Johnson, what was a matter of conscience for King was clear betrayal. J. Edgar Hoover had publicly attacked King on several occasions and was more than ready to reemploy the formula that had proved so effective.

The formula is to set up a patsy as the assassin, arrange professionals to assassinate the target, and control the investigation to see that only the patsy is legally blamed. Hoover, as the longtime head of the FBI and dominant as the nation's chief law enforcement officer working in concert with Johnson who, as vice president who would succeed Kennedy as president, were in the ideal place to effectively carry out this strategy.

Using logical reasoning and based on my experience, I believe that Lee Harvey Oswald, Sirhan Sirhan, and James Earl Ray, all very ineffective losers not capable of pulling off the accomplishment with which they are credited, were all patsies. I suspect that all three events were choreographed and tightly controlled by Hoover, who saved his job, held for over fifty years, and was in turned protected by Johnson, who gained, and maintained, the presidency through the actions of his FBI director. It is plausible that, as Johnson and Hoover believed, the Kennedys planned to replace Johnson with another Southern senator and fire J. Edgar Hoover after the election. In their minds, they had to act before the Kennedys dumped them as a matter of survival. And they did. Do unto others before they do unto you!

Mothers and their children may sometimes be forgiven for their mistakes, but men in positions of great power are rarely forgiven for mistakes that create vulnerabilities. They are always surrounded by opportunists who search constantly for opportunities to exploit and bring them down.

PART 1

FINANCIAL LEVERAGE

Historic Adventures in Finance

How Businesses Are Financed: Then and Now

Capitalism is the economic system that uses wealth, capital, for the creation of more wealth. In the process, it efficiently produces and delivers goods and services to the consuming public. This is the theory.

Adam Smith is the philosopher and author *(The Wealth of Nations)* who articulated the theory of capitalism as a most efficient economic system. Market competition is supposed to be the great regulator. Companies that are the most efficient at producing products that meet market expectations will have the lowest costs and can sell at the lowest price. They, rather than their competition, are compensated by currency payment for meeting the needs and wants of the market at the lowest price. In the marketplace, only the fittest will survive. Repeated success in having consumers vote for a company's product in this arena will determine whether the company will be among the fittest who survive. Competitive success is vital.

The market votes with currency based on price and product satisfaction. The market eliminates the inefficient and those whose products do not meet expectations. When the products do not sell because they are too costly or not acceptable for whatever reason, revenues will be insufficient to sustain the company. It will fail and be eliminated from market competition. Competition, the great market regulator, has performed its function. This is the theory underlying support for capitalism as an economic system.

There are those who say that when allowed to operate unfettered by the government, capitalistic societies quickly evolve into oligarchies that work overtime to eliminate their competition and create effective monopolies that prevent the entry or survival of competitors. This is what the communists attack as "monopoly capitalism." Teddy Roosevelt said, in reference to American antitrust laws designed to prevent monopolies, that if America was going to have big businesses, then it needed an even bigger government to control them. Roosevelt was known as the great "trust buster" who would bust apart monopoly trusts.

There are critics who claim that most large American markets are dominated by a small group of large companies, and it is foolish to believe that they do not get together informally at private places and conspire to protect their economic interest at the expense of the consuming public. It is even more foolish to believe that they do not make large campaign contributions to politicians to assist them in protecting their effective monopolies. They also pay powerful, well-connected lobbyists to manage their relationships with the government agencies to ease their regulations.

My experience is that the paranoia of these companies can extend even to businessmen engaged in starting up small businesses. I have seen them identify and work vigorously behind the scenes using the illegal and corrupt practices of key government officials. They have access to these connections only because of their wealth and position. They are fully capable of and willing to use any corrupt means to prevent the survival of what is only a potential competitor. Their prey, many times a struggling small business startup entrepreneur, can never know the real reason for the failure of the business. Invariably, the belief is that it was the entrepreneur's own inadequacies, never realizing that powerful forces saw to it that he or she never had a chance. The entrepreneur was honest and assumed everyone else was honest as well, never even contemplating that he or she was the victim of nefarious activity. This is how effective monopolies are maintained. More on this later.

Sources of Capital

Capitalism requires capital, wealth, to initiate and maintain activity and operations. Where can capitalists, especially small business entrepreneurs, gain access to the capital required for success? I remember the comment

If you are undercapitalized, there is almost no way you can succeed, and if you are overcapitalized, there is almost no way you will fail because you can then get past the learning curve and survive the small business startup chasm. Crossing the chasm is difficult because you are invisible to the market, visible prey to your competitors, and searching for a path to cross over the chasm to a solid foundation.

Historically, in Europe, it was "Old World control by the manor house." This was the basis of the European system. As part of Europe's reawakening during the Renaissance, merchants began to expand their operations and used corporate entities to raise funds. The European model depended heavily on going to the sovereign or large holders of wealth to seek backing. Typically, the monarchy or the manor house was petitioned to provide charters, concessions, and/or capital in the large amounts necessary for what were perceived as profitable ventures. Queen Isabella, a Hispanic woman, is reported to have sold her jewels to provide Columbus with the capital he needed to discover the New World in the fifteenth century. This venture by a Spanish monarch yielded amounts of gold from the New World that would exceed the wildest expectations.

Although new corporate financing instruments, such as stocks and bonds, were being used by merchants in Amsterdam and London, the usual expectation was to seek large sums from wealthy benefactors.

The Genius of American Corporate Capitalism

Although some Americans used similar means throughout the Gilded Age to seek financing from large monopoly trusts operated by anonymous investors, Americans pioneered taking a relatively small amount of money from a lot of people. One dollar is not a lot capital, but $1 from a million people is a million dollars. The post-World War II housing boom would take this model to a magnificent level.

Relative Wealth of American Households in a 1974 Federal Reserve Report

American Government Budget	$108 Billion
Combined State and Municipal Governments	$104 Billion
The Rest of the World	$224 Billion
Insurance Companies	$23 Billion
Pension Plans	$27 Billion
American Households	**$1.7 Trillion**

In 1974, American households are believed to have represented the greatest accumulation of wealth that had ever existed in the history of the world. This is the economic base underlying America's wealth-making power. America's wealth was, and still may be, the most powerful driving force for capital formation on the planet.

Capital Formation: Debt versus Equity

Capital is invested in two fundamental ways. Money is invested in equity ownership or through debt instruments. An investor purchases equity as a proprietor, stockholder, partner, or hybrid security. An investor may also acquire debt instruments that pay interest for the use of the money. Equity and debt instruments can be structured in limitless variations. Both stock and debt instruments can be structured to be preferred as to right and time for distribution of income and options to be cumulative and/or participate with common stock dividends or be distributed in any other variation agreed upon.

Corporate Finance

Fundamentally, a corporation is a legal entity, not a natural person, who is chartered to exist by the state. The filing of articles of incorporation, once accepted and certified by the state, represents the corporation's birth certificate. It is a legal person and has the same rights as any citizen as described in the Fourteenth Amendment to the United States Constitution. The Fourteenth Amendment states that no state may deny any person (that means legal or natural) due process of law. Corporations are entitled to the equal protection of the law.

A corporation is owned and controlled by its shareholders. Shareholders buy the corporation's capital stock to provide funds for the corporation to operate. Those who buy common stock are entitled to vote to elect the board of directors who make policy for, and control, the business of the corporation. A corporation can only act through its agents. The board of directors elects, virtually hiring, the president, the treasurer, and the secretary. As structures have gotten more complicated, the offices are now referred to as the chief executive officer, the chief financial officer, and the chief operating officer, and as many corporate vice presidents as, in the opinion of the board of directors, the organization requires. These rules are set out in the corporate bylaws adopted by the board of directors. The state law sets forth the power of the shareholders, but its primary power is to elect the directors who have the support of the shareholders. During an annual meeting, the shareholders can, pursuant to the bylaws, elect new directors to replace those in whom they have lost confidence.

A corporation may have more than one class of capital stock. It may issue preferred stock to a different class of investors who are assured of a preferred return before other classes of stock. In years when the income may be inadequate to permit a distribution to common stockholders, the requirements of the preference may nevertheless require funds be distributed to the preferred stockholders. They may even be given voting rights with the common stockholders. The general understanding, however, is that common stockholders vote on management and preferred stockholders have a payment preference, but the possible variations are endless.

Sources of Corporate Capital

To initiate and maintain operations, businesses need capital. Normally, most small businesses look to create a relationship with a commercial bank. Once they have ongoing relationships with suppliers and other vendors, they can establish trade credit on an ongoing basis. Commercial banks make it clear that they lend to customers who can use credit, not to customers who need credit. Invariably, to sustain growth, more sources will be necessary. Most successful businesses will eventually hire attorneys who have relationships with investment bankers that open doors to the equity and debt markets in addition to venture capital and private equity.

Cash Flow Dedicated as Capital

Very successful corporations can sustain some growth through cash flow earnings. There are no broker's fees, points, or interest associated with these funds. The corporation needs no government approvals and can act on its own initiative. This is now free money over which the corporation exercises exclusive control.

Corporate Debt Finance

Stockholder dividends are rights to income arising from a declaration of the board of directors that allow stockholder to share in the business profits of the corporation. This decision to declare a stock income dividend is discretionary with the board of directors.

Payment of debt, however, is not discretionary. All debt is based on a promise to pay. Generally, in full at maturity with periodic payments until maturity. This promise to pay is contained in a debt instrument referred to as a promissory note that generally promises the face amount of the promissory note along with interest as rent for the use of the money at a specific rate for a specific time. All debt instruments are a variation on a promissory note. Two of the most important are commercial paper and corporate bonds.

Commercial papers are negotiable instruments issued by creditworthy corporations promising to pay a specific amount at a date certain, generally ninety days into the future. They are generally sold at a discount that will convert at maturity into a return based upon a return of interest. A company with cash flow issues can issue these notes for immediate cash and repay with receivables that come in. These smooth out the highs and lows of cash flows and provide a source of income for company with idle cash.

Corporations, when in need of long-term financing, will issue promissory notes in smaller amounts to make them easier to sell. Rather than seeking one lender to loan $100,000 to be repaid according to the terms of a promissory note, the corporation can instead issue one hundred bonds, which are promissory notes for $1,000 each. It is easier to find one hundred people with $1,000 that it is to find one person with $100,000 that is willing to lend. Many times, bond programs will have a stockbrokerage to act as a bond manager and administer the program in manner designed to protect the interest of individual bond holders.

Sometimes bonds are convertible, meaning that they can be converted to stock upon the occurrence of specified events and pursuant to specified terms that were set when the bonds were issued.

The Importance of Corporate Credit Ratings

The big issue with a corporate bond is its credit rating. In theory, credit rating agencies evaluate their financial strength using both information that they ascertained privately and information available to the public. The best rating, depending on the service, is A or AAA, and these are considered investment grade. This mean that fiduciaries, people who are legally bound to work only in the best interest of their clients rather than themselves, can recommend these securities as safe investments without fear of regulatory action or punishment. Because these are considered safe, the issuers can sell them while paying the lowest interest rate. Because of the safety, there are buyers even if the interest may be higher elsewhere. Interest rate return is governed by the degree of perceived risk represented by the instrument. Stockbrokers and certified investment advisors can only recommend and sell investments, stocks and bonds, that are investment grade. When interest rates are very low, investors tend to look for alternative investments, such as real estate or precious metals, for a higher rate with comparable safety.

Finance is a very dynamic industry that can reward creative innovators, but also subject them to cruel reprisals from both competitors and those whose interest they may be affecting adversely.

Leveraged Buyout (LBO) Innovation

An interesting LBO story is one analysis concerning how bonds that were not investment grade went from being referred to as "junk bonds" to "high-yield bonds." A brilliant innovator devised a system to allow a company's executives to buy the entire company by leveraging the company's assets. They would offer to shareholders a high price for their stock on condition that they have the company issue bonds that company's income would repay, but the bond proceeds would be used to pay for the stock purchase buying out the existing shareholders. Because of the high degree of leverage, the company's financial strength was spent after the buyout and the bonds has a low value far below investment grade. Hence, they earned the name "junk bonds." An ambitious US attorney saw a chance to make a name for himself by suing and prosecuting the innovative financier who had come up with the idea and who made enormous amounts of money funding these deals. He found investors who were willing to invest in junk. The US attorney assumed someone was being defrauded and built a case using securities law claiming the innovation was a scam. The innovator started making enormous amounts of money and mounted a campaign daring the US attorney to go to trial. In the end, a deal was struck whereby the innovator pleaded guilty to minor items and spent eighteen months in a comfortable prison with the atmosphere of a country club.

Then something interesting happened. Whereas investment-grade bonds were paying about 2 percent interest, junk bonds, because they were perceived to present a great deal of risk, paid 9 percent interest. But then 98 percent of the junk bonds paid off as agreed. Investors quickly realized that they could invest in junk bonds and have 2 percent of them fail and still come out with an overall return of 7 percent rather than the 2 percent paid by investment-grade bonds. Junk bonds then became high-yield bonds. There are mutual funds that buy them using strategies of extreme diversification and do quite well. They are not highly invested in any one issue and assume that 2 percent will fail. But practice has shown that, as a class, these bonds are resilient.

The innovator, however, is now stigmatized as a convicted felon and can never deal in securities again. He has been legally banned from involvement with securities for the rest of his life.

He was sufficiently wealthy to start a medical research foundation and has remained somewhat relevant to the world, but the incredible innovations he made in the field of corporate finance have had to move on without his genius and creativity.

The Role of Bankers: Money Brokers

What a difference forty years makes in commercial banking. In 1982, I led a group of professionals in applying to the Office of the Controller of the Currency for a charter to form a national bank. We were successful, and I then received a unique education.

Banking as we understood it at that time was dependent upon the professionalism of experienced bankers who could evaluate the "three Cs" concerning the bank's customers. When a businessperson comes in for a loan, a banker must determine whether he has the character, capacity, and collateral the bank wants to see. Is he a person of good character who pays his bills, and does he have the capacity to work his way out of the kind of trouble that all businesspeople encounter? Finally, does he have the collateral to guarantee that the bank will be paid when all else falls?

After receiving our charter and raising the funds to start operations, we purchased a banking temple, at an excellent location, from an established bank. In the process, I became acquainted with the established bank's CEO. He confided to me that he had learned that banking is people, it depends on the skills of people, and that he hoped that he never forgets that banking is people.

He would not recognize banking today. The role of people at the retail level is shrinking. Today banking is governed by credit scores, credit and debit cards, and computerized algorithms that make the lending decisions. Banking is now artificial intelligence, computer decisions, and customer service phone operators. The three Cs are no longer relevant.

Over 100 million Americans have substandard credit. Fair credit starts with a score of about 630, good credit starts at 680, and excellent credit at 750. Living with poor credit can be very difficult.

Many businesses will do business with persons having fair credit, but poor credit is a real problem for many people.

Your credit score and bank policy determine your credit card lending limit. Individual credit decisions are made by computers following predetermined algorithms programmed into systems with more and more reliance upon artificial intelligence capability. People are just aides and facilitators in the bank's marketing and administration.

Personal Credit Management

The key strategic capability in society today is to be able to manage, improve, and maintain one's credit score. Excellent credit opens doors and goes everywhere, and bad credit struggles to survive. An education I received from an organization called the Best Bank Method run by a former FICO employee, Steve Snyder, is the only program I have found that actually delivers on being able to meaningfully assist in personal credit management and improvement. There are dozens of programs that advertise that they can improve credit scores, but I have found most to be worthless and ineffective. Many, including banks, claimed to provide me with my credit score. To my amazement, I have found them to be inaccurate and possibly fraudulent.

There are three important credit reporting agencies. They are Equifax, TransUnion, and Experian. But they only report credit information; they do not issue scores. Scores are issued by Fair Isaac Corporation, also known as FICO. By law, the reporting agencies are required to make your report available to you once a year at no cost. However, this does not include credit scores. I would go on Google to get my credit score and it would light up with offers of free reports. These were lies. When I would go to a site, there was always a charge. Nothing was free with the advertised reporting services, only the misinformation and lies. The one truly free legally required site did not seem to advertise. It was www.annualcreditreport.com.

It turns out that today, in the year 2023, there are only two ways to get your actual credit score. One is to buy a home with a loan secured by a mortgage. By law, the lender must provide your actual credit score upon which the loan is being made.

The second method is hiring a credit reporting agency to monitor you credit reports and score. Fair Isaac Corporation provides this service called myFico. "myFico member services" include updates of your FICO Scores and credit report.

The myFico service also offers simulations that allow a member to do what-if simulations to see what effect different payments for different time periods will have on your credit scores. You can calculate the payment you need to make and the number of months it will take to improve your score and achieve your desired status.

Business Credit Issues

The Business Personal Guarantee: The Companion Problems of the Personal Guarantee and Mortgaging a Home to Guarantee Payment of a Business Debt

When I began in business, I needed financing. The only sources I knew of were banks and government agencies. The banking counselors advised me concerning the importance of the three Cs of character, capacity, and collateral. I had to show that I was worthy of their trust. When I applied for a loan guaranteed by the US government's Small Business Administration, I was required to put my home up as collateral. When I objected, I was told that if I did not have enough confidence to mortgage my own home, why should the lender have confidence that I would pay as agreed? I had to earn the trust of the lender with my character and my willingness to my put my home on the line. It was all on me and if I didn't measure up in either way, then I wasn't worthy of their assistance. So my path to financing my business required a personal guarantee from me and a lien on my home. This was the cost of obtaining financing if I wanted to go into business for myself. When challenged, I agreed, and it worked out for me. It is fundamental with banks and the SBA that all borrowers sign a personal guarantee and mortgage any property they own.

Small Business Corporate Business Credit as Opposed to Personal Credit and Personal Guarantees

Now older, and I believe far wiser, I know there are options that I was not aware of in my youth. First, a reality check. Most businesses fail. SBA statistics indicate that 80 percent of new business fail within the first five years of operations. The implication is that approximately 80 percent of the time, a personal guarantee and mortgage lien will lead to homelessness, bankruptcy, and a learning experience from which few can recover.

Today, my advice is to never sign a personal guarantee for business debt. Structure the business debt so that the business can stand on its own.

Small Business Corporate Business Credit

Business credit is based upon a company's prompt payment of trade credit and the company's DUNS score issued by Dun & Bradstreet. If a business is prompt in trade payments to its suppliers and vendors, it can maintain a high score. Once seasoned, this score can back business credit cards given to the business. Whereas personal credit cards may allow a maximum balance of about $5,000, business credit typically will go to $25,000 and it is not uncommon for business to have four to six of them. These require no personal guarantee. They represent credit given to the business for promptly paying its bills. It is possible, therefore, for a business owner to have over $100,000 in unsecured credit without having to sign a personal guarantee. Business credit is not available for a startup. It must be earned by the business over time with good bill paying performance. Startups will go through a learning curve and must prove their fitness to survive and prosper.

How to Approach a Startup

Chances for survival increase exponentially if the entrepreneurs have several years of relevant experience and learned their skills working in a similar business. Furthermore, add to this a detailed business plan like the franchise example described the book *The E-Myth*. Finally, do not commence operations until unencumbered funds, sufficient to conveniently cover anticipated losses in addition to potential unpleasant surprises, have been accumulated and dedicated to the venture. Expect to sustain at least a year of significant negative cash flows.

I remember an experienced entrepreneur stating, "What I have found is that there is almost no way a business can survive if it is undercapitalized and almost no way it can fail if it is overcapitalized."

If the entrepreneur has no unencumbered funds or other resources to dedicate to the business for startup capital, the entrepreneur must recognize that there is a problem. Problem recognition is the first phase of problem-solving. Using the protocols set forth in the book *Make Luck Happen*, I have been solving these kinds of problems for years. At first approach, it always seems impossible. You must think about it, search for opportunities, and prepare your capability to seized them. It is a lot of challenging work, but doable.

When I used to meet with individuals who wanted to be my partners, I would sit down and go over what needed to be done to verify the business opportunity, to develop the plan, and to raise the funds needed. It was a massive amount of work. The typical feedback was "We need the funds first to pay *someone else* to do this work. So *you* get the money and come back so that *we* can spend it." It took a while, but eventually I learned to move forward alone. Now I will make luck happen to find the startup funds. My rules now are not to take investor money, not to sell securities, and not to borrow money without proven sources of repayment already in hand. With no funds in hand, no initial idea of how to get it, and my rules on what not to do, that is how I define the problem. I will now use the protocols in the book *Make Luck Happen* to find the solution.

A prescription for disaster is an inexperienced entrepreneur wannabe seeking to start a business gambling on success with someone else's money.

A well-capitalized, experienced entrepreneur attempting to seize a viable business opportunity using a financially feasible business plan detailed like a franchise coupled with a trained, motivated workforce is needed to competently attempt the startup of a new venture.

Registered versus Exempted Securities

Serious issues they don't teach you in school. Most people do not realize that as the laws are written, any investment contract where money is paid with the expectation that it will be returned with a profit is a security. It is against the law to offer or transfer any security unless it has been registered with the Securities and Exchange Commission and the local state securities regulation agency. Federal registration takes about nine months and several hundred thousand dollars to accomplish. If an issuer transfers ownership of an unregistered security, it is a criminal offense that can lead to a felony conviction.

So any person who sells an ownership interest in any business without first registering with the Securities and Exchange Commission and the California Corporation Commission's Office of Business Oversite, for California residents, has committed two felonies, one federal and one state, for which they could be sentenced to state and/or federal prison.

The keys for the small businesspersons are transactions that are exempt from the law. At the federal level, the private placement must not advertise, there must be a private placement memorandum disclosing all the risk factors and other pertinent information providing full disclosure of material facts, and these private securities are offered and sold only to persons with whom the issuer already has a business relationship where potential investors have had an opportunity to gauge the issuer's business acumen. This then may qualify as a private offering that is exempt from registration. States have similar exemptions. Another exemption from the federal law is the intrastate exemption whereby all events, players, and assets are within the boundaries of a single state.

The Dangers of Exemptions

Exemptions are a trap for the talented entrepreneur, especially minorities, starting a business. Exemption law is very technical, and each element must be complied with exactly, or it fails. One requirement is that you disclose all material facts in your offering circular. However, this is an effective impossibility. Prosecutors and aggrieved investors will always find an obscure fact that was not fully disclosed, and this will cause the exemption to fail. Good-faith attempts are not a defense; they only mean that the entrepreneur did not comply. Now the entrepreneur is a felon for transferring an unregistered security that turned out not to be exempt. His or her good-faith effort to comply with the law has just sent the entrepreneur to prison and made the entrepreneur a criminal.

As a practical matter, if everything goes as planned and everyone's expectation as to the return is fulfilled, no one complains and everything is fine. But we know that about 80 percent of the time, thing don't go well. Many investors believe that if things go well, it is because they were smart investors. If they do not go well, it is because the promoting entrepreneur is a crook. They then want blood and will complain to law enforcement and cooperate fully in testifying to whatever they need to say to convict even the well-meaning honest entrepreneur (who they feel stole their money).

An Effective Weapon for Competitors

Where this gets seriously dangerous is when a competitor realizes the potential of this weapon. It is a simple, but amazingly effective, strategy to make, or arrange, sizable contributions to a district attorney's political reelection campaign. The competitor then has access to the prosecutor to complain about the entrepreneur's alleged criminal behavior. The least the prosecutor can do is initiate an investigation. Although it will go unsaid, future financial support from the competitor will depend upon the how vigorous the DA pursues the prosecution. Since all the prosecutors need to do is find an obscure fact that the entrepreneur did not disclose, there is a good possibility that there will be a successful persecution and prosecution.

One example involved an innovative city planning commissioner who wanted to assess fast-food corporations to help pay for low-income housing. One fast-food corporation operated nationally. It reasoned that if one city succeeded in imposing this burden, others may follow. What until then seemed unimportant became very important when it would potentially affect the national market. The local district attorney, at the urgent request of the fast-food corporation, investigated the low-cost housing program and found that funds were invested based upon an exemption from securities registration. The planning commissioner was a sponsor of the project and a promoter. The DA charged him with selling an unregistered security. He was forced to enter a plea bargain where he spent no time in jail, finished returning all funds to his investors, which he had agreed to do anyway, and entered into plea bargain where he pleaded guilty to a technical securities fraud. The DA and the fast-food corporation did not care whether he went to jail; they just wanted him, and his ideas, killed off politically. But the entrepreneur is a convicted felon and was automatically disbarred from the practice of law.

Small businesspersons seldom realize how seriously their actions are taken by their competition or the weapons that are available to competitors who can, and will, pay for the entrepreneur's demise.

Important Sidenote

The effect this experience had on the defendant entrepreneur was to induce a mental illness in the form of an obscure depression and debilitating anxiety. Years later while still suffering from the condition, he happened to see the 1957 movie *The Wrong Man* starring Henry Fonda, who plays an innocent person whose eyewitnesses against him were pressured by police to identify him as the criminal. The defendant's wife experienced extreme helplessness just as the entrepreneur had felt when others had control of his defense. She became mentally ill and exhibited symptoms that the entrepreneur recognized in himself. The movie had a Hollywood ending. The innocent person was exonerated, and the wife recovered after two years in a mental hospital. The entrepreneur, who had now suffered for years with anxiety and depression, researched the film's original story to get the name of the condition so that he could seek help for himself. The real story was that the wife never recovered and died after a few years in the hospital. The powerful persecution of an innocent person by the criminal justice system resulted in her death. The entrepreneur attempted anew to avoid this end. After over twenty years of suffering and just existing as a person, he regained his swagger and started fighting back. However, his analysis and memories disclosed a phenomenon that he found extremely disturbing. The cause of his illness was not so much the criminal prosecution but treatment he received from his defense attorneys.

The entrepreneur, a trained, experienced attorney, found that there are four conflicts of interest that have corrupted the criminal legal system and there is no one to address them. No one has, or wants, to recognize the problem. Describing all four is the subject of a separate treatise; at this time, I will only discuss the one currently relevant.

The defense attorney, and that of the codefendant, never ceased preaching that the criminal justice system was stacked against the defendant. The cost of an effective defense was beyond the financial means of most defendants. Most judges accept the word of police and prosecutors who lie all the time. The investigators for the district attorney break the law and use illegal means all the time, and no one in authority cares because it makes conviction of the bad guys easier. Although all men are presumed innocent, as a practical matter, it is just the opposite. The defendant's word doesn't count because he has been charged. Now his word doesn't count and should never be believed.

What they preached was helplessness and dependence on the defense attorney. The defense attorney's primary interest is how much money they can extort from their client. *The defense attorney's business model is to scare the defendant out of all the money they have or can get from friends and relatives, then enter a plea deal so that their work is done.*

All other parties go along with it because it makes their job easier. The result is not their responsibility. The system overwhelms the judges with the enormous number of cases they need to pass on judicially. These plea deals make life much easier and prevent the system from collapsing.

The defense attorney preaches constantly that they are the defendant's only chance, but only after they have paid the attorney all they have. The judges, they say, rarely take motions seriously. Few judges bother to read pleadings in detail. It is easier not to buck the police and prosecutors, whom they must live with, than to take up the cause of some defendant who is probably guilty anyway.

Eventually, the constant preaching by the defense attorney has its effect and a depression, which can lead to severe mental illness, can set in with the defendant who feels helpless and cornered. A former prison inmate once told me that he observed prison inmates exhibit these symptoms of depression and anxiety.

If you are innocent, helpless, and persecuted, this is what happens to you.

Business Law and the Legal Environment

The stock market abuses of the 1920s and the crash of '29 that led to the Great Depression mandated that government do something to prevent the dangerous overleverage and abuse of margin loans, blatant fraud, and greedy deceptions and secret manipulations by powerful unknown forces.

The result was the Securities Exchange Act of 1933 followed by another act in 1934 that regulated investment banking. There were more regulatory laws to follow so that banking, specifically investment banking, commercial banking, and mortgage banking, all became among the most regulated of industries. The states enacted blue-sky laws to regulate the sale of securities within their jurisdictions. Some followed the federal disclosure model, and others, like California, require a permit to sell stock, but the permit is only issued after the Corporation Commission's Office of Business Oversite determines that the offering is fair, just, and equitable. Disclosure only is not enough.

The 1934 act created the Securities and Exchange Commission to oversee the industry. Stockbrokers and investment firms are licensed under its authority. The commission monitors the markets and enforces securities laws.

Section 10 B and rule 10b-5 of the '34 act prohibit what some bankers do best: *cheat.* Some bankers appear to make money by knowing how and when to manipulate and cheat. Ivan Boesky, the high-end investment banker who went to jail for insider trading and served as the inspiration for the movie *Wall Street,* had the ability to secretly secure and use inside information. Is he an isolated example who happened to get caught, or is he just the tip of the iceberg? In the movie *Hustlers,* the actress JLo has a scene where she describes high-end banker clients at her strip club. "The very successful that run the firms cheat the little people all day long and into the night." Among the greed, expertise, and power of bankers at the highest levels and the powerful tools available to regulators, the small businessperson and the small investors are outmaneuvered and operate in the financial world at a great disadvantage.

Four films seemed to capture the dark side of banking culture. These are *Wall Street, Hustlers,* the sequel to *Wall Street* entitled *Wall Street: Money Never Sleeps,* and *The Big Short.* They provide a very practical education.

How Startup Financing with Investment Bankers Works for a Small Business Entrepreneur: "Real-Life Experience, Not Theory"

My early experiences with high-profile investment banking firms made me decide to make them irrelevant. I was building an apartment project and needed financing. I went to them for assistance. They viewed my request, to have my project considered for funding by them, as absurd. An inexperienced, minority entrepreneur with no track record requesting money from high-level investment banking firms was the worst of all bad jokes. I was rejected, mocked, and insulted as I was shown the exit door. Years later, with my now somewhat impressive track record, they would call soliciting my business and I would answer, "Who needs you now? When I needed you, you showed me the exit. I now return the favor."

The fastest way to money is not fast, and unless you are prequalified, it is not through bankers. Doing it on your own takes time, but it is possible. And for those without resources, experience, or wealthy family and friends, it may be the only way.

Falling back upon my political experience, I realized that these bankers were not the source of financial power but were a symptom of it. The sources were the individual investors who lived in those American households described in the 1974 Federal Reserve report. The bankers were the brokers in between. So I analyzed. I went to law school. I thought, *I will research what they do, learn it, and do it myself. I will bypass them and go directly to the source of power.*

I immediately discovered that people tend to be lazy and would rather someone else do it for them. To make use of the opportunity presented by the wealth of American household, I came upon the following realization: If I ask a lot of friends and relatives for amounts that they are comfortable with, there was a good chance some would say yes. I could also test the laziness and commitment of some of my wannabe partners in this business promotion.

$100,000 is a lot for one person to invest. But $100 is not a prohibitive amount. So are we willing to seek $100 from one thousand people? It is doable, but it is a lot of work. When I would present it as pathway to success to my partners and promotion associates, the answer was "You go out and get the money so we can spend it." When I insisted that they do their share, the response was "It is an unreasonable impossible task." I agreed with them. For them it was impossible, but I was not going to let others determine my fate negatively.

So I moved on alone and would only consider as future associates and partners those who came to me and showed proper motivation. I would consider those who, when I described the enormity of the venture's obligation, would answer, "I am ready, willing, and able to try, but I don't know how. Will you teach me?" I then handed them a copy of my paper on how. See my paper "How to Raise Money by Selling Securities Privately" below. We would then follow SEC guidelines and prepare the offering circular, the private placement memorandum.

How to Raise Money by Selling Securities Privately

It is imperative that one understands the very real dangers of issuing securities. Most people have no idea of the nature or depth of the risk. Most lawyers are ill-equipped to advise on this subject, and the securities specialists who do know are too expensive and inaccessible to be of service to the average person. Furthermore, their honest advice would be that the cards are stacked against you and overzealous regulators, with the powerful weapons they can deploy, can destroy you.

Nevertheless, for those intrepid souls who, like the crew of the *Pequod* whaling ship in the novel *Moby Dick* are willing to assume the risk (incidentally, only one survived), I will describe how I used to do it before the ship fell apart.

Begin by assuming that all passive investment contracts, where the money does the work and the buyers are passive investors, are securities and are regulated by both the federal and state governments. The general rule is that it is a felony crime to issue and sell a security unless it has been registered with the federal Securities and Exchange Commission and a permit has been issued by the state regulatory authorities. It takes hundreds of thousands of dollars in professional fees and almost a year generally to secure such registration and permits.

There are, however, certain securities that are exempt from such registration. Most small issuers rely on one or more of these exemptions. The problem with these exemptions, however, is that absolute compliance is required, or you have committed a crime. Good-faith, reasonable efforts are not enough. It you don't, for whatever reason, meet the exact requirements, the exemption fails and you can be successfully prosecuted for a felony.

As a practical matter, what this means is that if some investors are unhappy, they can go to enforcement authorities to complain. It also means that competitors have an effective means to mount secret attacks by means of stealth and through conspiring third parties. The authorities, if they decide that the case meets their priorities, can always find a fact that can invalidate the exemption and put the issuer in jail. One of the requirements is that full disclosure of all risks is required. If a risk is not disclosed, the private placement memorandum is fraudulent. Enforcement officials can always find an obscure risk that no one thought of and that was overlooked. They can then successfully allege fraud, invalidate the exemption, and make the issuer a criminal. The common law concept of Scienter, an intent to defraud, required for an action in deceit, common law fraud, is not required in securities law. It is literally strict liability; either you meet the requirements of the exemption or you are guilty of a criminal offense. These laws can, and are, frequently abused. An unfortunate and innocent businessman who has enemies either at the chamber of commerce or at city hall can quickly find himself in jail and his life and career ruined.

For some, the need for capital is such that they decide to assume the risks and go forward with issuing securities.

One method, which has been successfully utilized to raise money by selling securities, is set forth below.

An offering circular is created. One commonly used exemption is the private placement exemption. This requires a disclosure document referred to as private placement memorandum that is supposed to disclose the assumptions upon which the financial projections are based, an explanation of the venture being embarked upon, the experience and qualifications of the venture's management personnel, and a full disclosure of the risks to which the investment capital will be exposed.

From a marketing perspective, I have found that this document can never state, but must imply, that it is a "sure thing, can't miss" business. This is the feeling the investor must have after reviewing the document. If all the risks that they can think of have been addressed to their satisfaction, they will say that the presentation is nice, but they will not invest. What is needed is that the documents leave them feeling that there is no way, if they do invest, that they can lose money. If this is accomplished, then the foundation has been laid for the next phase. This next phase is referred to as "big bucks." If one starts with big bucks, it come across as "pie in the sky" fantasy. However, if the foundation has been laid and the potential investor has reached the point where he or she believes they won't lose money, they then can reason that if the investment performs as presented, they will be something close to rich. Then the greed factor kicks in and they can see themselves spending the money they are going to make as they decide to write a check. So the foundation is "sure thing, can't miss" and the motivator is "big bucks."

Once the presentation documents have been prepared, the next step is to develop a list of potential investors. When I contact them, I don't request that they invest. Rather, I always say that I have an investment that I think may interest someone they know. I ask to show it to them to get their opinion and a referral. I never put them into a position of having to say no. I value their opinion, and some of their friends may appreciate the opportunity. I try to get three referrals I can contact.

I assume that if I can get one purchaser for each ten presentations that I make, I will be doing well.

Most programs, when I was doing them, were for $500,000 and are limited by law to thirty-five investors. So I am looking to sell thirty-five shares at $14,280 each. I am prepared to make 350 presentations, one every day or night for a year if necessary. What generally happens is that after a presentation, a person will say, "I would be interested, and I think some of my friends would also be interested." That is when sales begin. At first, it will go slow, but as I make presentations, I recognize what the prospects are sensitive to and what sells. My presentations get better. I may start out at one out of ten, but I quickly get to the point where I am closing eight or nine out of ten. I have never had to make more than fifty presentations before I have sold thirty-five shares and raised $500,000.

Being sold is one thing; staying sold is something else. Customer relations and constant communication during, especially during the early stages, is important. As the venture is successful, the success speaks volumes for you. If there are problems, the need for communications is important. People tend to feel that if the venture is successful, it is because they are smart investors. If it is not, it is because the promoters are crooks. Constant full disclosure where they understand all that is happening prevents unpleasant surprises. Some may demand their money back. Do so immediately if possible. If not, then consult your attorneys who will soon need to deal with other attorneys and/or enforcement officials.

Real Estate Finance

First some fundamentals and historical sidenotes.

Buy land: They are not making any more of it. Land is central to human existence and sustenance. With workable and accessible land, man has a place to live and grow food. Infrastructure makes land accessible for human use and enjoyment. Modern appliances enable productive use of the opportunities found on the land.

Access to land is worthless without access to water, roads, electricity, ports, labor, talent, capital, raw materials, and real estate professions. The value of land depends on who owns it. The value comes from what is done to it that gives it value. Some developers are more effective than others in this respect.

Land as a Factor in American History

Native Americans were the first victims. They sided with the British during the Revolutionary War. During the negotiations for peace, the British tried to arrange a land for the Native Americans, and the Americans would have none of it. Again, during negotiations to end the War of 1812, the British wanted to reserve all land west of the Appalachian Mountains for a Native American state, and again, the Americans wanted that land for their White people. When Andrew Jackson became president 1828, he supported laws to remove the Indians to the Indian Territory in what is now Oklahoma. The US Supreme Court ruled in favor of the Indigenous cause, and Andrew Jackson refused to uphold the decision. The Native Americans were removed, and many died in transit on the Trail of Tears. But the White people got their land. As it turns out, the elites were also doing similar things in the British Isles. Note a comparison of the events in Scotland and the American South.

The theorical foundation of capitalism is set forth in a book written in the eighteenth century. A Scotsman named Adam Smith wrote *The Wealth of Nations* and, as part of his investigation into the wealth of nations, set forth the essential doctrines of capitalism. To my surprise when I read it, it turns out Adam Smith was concerned about the plight of poor people and gives a look at what it looked like in the 1700s. In his work, he writes,

> Poverty, though it does not prevent the generation, is extremely unfavourable to the rearing of children [...] It is not uncommon [...] in the Highlands of Scotland for a mother who has borne twenty children not to have two alive [...] In some places one half the children born die before they are four years of age; in many places before they are seven; and in almost all places before they are nine or ten. This great mortality, however, will everywhere be found chiefly among the children of the common people, who cannot afford to tend them with the same care as those of better station.

But there were other events taking place in the Scottish Highlands during the 1700s that would be repeated in America over the next century. During treaty negotiations to end the American Revolution, and again to end the War of 1812, the British tried to gain land for Native Americans. The Americans, represented by the new nation's elite, would hear none of it. They would yield no land to the Indians. Within a decade, they forcibly evicted the Indians from their land in the South. The Indians were forced into the Trail of Tears, where 25 percent of them died of starvation and exposure while walking to the Indian Territory in Oklahoma.

This was similar what the elites in the British Isles were doing in the Scottish Highlands. There, the elites had learned that sheep herding was more profitable than renting to the Highlander families. So clans that had occupied lands for over five hundred years were being evicted from their ancestral homes. As noted above, many were poor and starvation become common. They either found homes or were shipped, sometimes by their landlords, to the Americas. With no remorse and operating pursuant to the law of jungle's survival of the fittest, the wealthy in both Scotland and the American South began to take land from the weak and poor. The removals cleared the Scottish Highlands of people primarily to allow for the introduction of sheep pastoralism. Expansion of the White-owned slave cotton culture was a motivation in the American South. In both cases, it was all legally sanctioned by the prevailing law. Both the Scottish Highlanders and the American Indians were poor and politically weak, and both suffered the same fate in losing what land, position, power, and wealth they had.

I am struck by the differences in eighteenth-century morals, laws, and culture and those existing today. Eighteenth-century elites had no problem viewing the world as a survival of the fittest being natural norm. Today, since the inception of the New Deal, government has stepped in to assist the poor. But always over strenuous opposition. Today, there are still those who want to turn back the clock and dismantle the safety net for the poor the government has erected. If the elites of the eighteenth century had no issue with the poor dying of starvation when it was in their interest, is it any wonder that the elites of today would further their interest despite the mass number of deaths caused by tobacco use or use of fossil fuels that intensifies global warming?

The United States convinced France to bankrupt itself supporting the American Revolution, then snubbed France so that it could not attend treaty negotiations to recoup some of its expenditures. Soon after, during the Napoleonic Wars, France needed money and sold its American holdings to the United States to raise cash. So America bankrupted them, leading to the French Revolution, then bought their American property in a distressed sale. The American public now had land to settle and upon which they could build a nation.

Jackson's protégé, President James Polk, arranged in 1847 for American forces to start a war with Mexico so that America could take land extending to the Pacific Ocean. The Americans negotiated an end-of-war treaty that they believed fulfilled America's Manifest Destiny. The United States stretched from the Atlantic to the Pacific, and all the land was opened to settlers. It was one of the world's greatest land grabs.

The Mexican War and the Louisiana Purchase represented land acquisitions by means that were less than honorable according to today's middle-class norms but made perfect sense when the moral compass dictated survival of the fittest. America got the land, so no one cared. Manifest Destiny was quite compatible with the law of the jungle.

But the land grabs were not over. When the Anglo White invasion of California took place during the gold rush of 1849, 90 percent of the Native American population was murdered as vermin, and the sources of Hispanic commerce, wealth, and economic power, the California hacienda system, created by land grants, were intentionally destroyed through utilization of a malicious tax system.

The traditional Hispanic tax system was to tax what the land produced, the food produced, the new livestock born each year, the number of cow hides exported, etc. These types of commerce and wealth were the basis for taxation. The Anglos arranged a Constitutional Convention in 1872, and under the new state constitution, they taxed pursuant to the English system that taxed the value of the land as determined by the local assessor. Because the haciendas included vast amounts of land, the numbers were astronomical. The only way a hacienda owner could pay his taxes was to sell half his entire estate. The Anglos bought at fire sale prices. Within ten years, being cut in half each year reduced the estates to insignificance.

Land as a Vehicle for Exploitation, Discrimination, and Persecution

Land can be used to exploit people to maintain, and profit from, privileged positions. In prerevolutionary Mexico in 1910, 90 percent of the land was owned by eighty-five families. The masses were unable to be landowners. No one would sell to them. Peonage, debt slavery, was the plight of most of the population. Eighty percent of the population was 100 percent Indian. The situation for former slaves, Black sharecroppers, was similar. Sharecroppers and peons found it impossible to get ahead of the wealth curve; they could not accumulate wealth. Everything is structured so that the cost of living exceeds income.

Land and finance can also be used to maintain privilege and unjustly ensure economic weakness of minority ethnic groups. At the turn of the nineteenth century, a family saved for years to assemble enough money to buy land and build a home. The amortized mortgage made it possible to pay off a loan in small payments over a period of thirty years. FHA would even go forty years. Amortized mortgages were made possible by the government programs of the Federal Housing Administration. An amortized loan promissory note secured by a deed of trust or mortgage allowed buyers to live in the house while saving to buy the home. A loan amortized over forty years meant that even the poor had a chance at homeownership. After World War II, veterans were able to get 100 percent loan to value loans. They did not have to produce a down payment.

However, there was one glaring issue. The programs were administered by White men who saw to it that loans would not go the Black families because of a practice called redlining, whereby certain "substandard" areas were to be avoided and any reason could be found not to lend. Lack of down payment funds, poor credit, lack of employment opportunities, and blatant discrimination meant that the suburban miracle of wealth accumulation and increased value through real estate would not, until the civil rights movement, be available to many Black people. The experience of slavery, the unfairness and hoarseness of a sharecropper economy, and redlining would mean that Black people would be several generations behind their White counterparts.

But the story is more than just one of lack of opportunity. Despite the discrimination and unfairness, some Black people were still able to prosper. Areas referred to as Black Wall Street grew in several towns throughout the South. The Carolinas, Georgia, and Florida all had such communities. The most prominent, however, was in Tulsa, Oklahoma. All these Black Wall Streets suffered the same fate. White supremacists, especially those envious of Black economic prosperity, would determine to attack and destroy a Black Wall Street and community. It would begin with a claim that Blacks had sexuality assaulted a White woman. Then it would go beyond the accusations and Whites would declare open season on Black people and their property. In Tulsa, even the White police and White elements of the armed forces participated in the attack, murdering and maiming Black people and burning their property.

Whenever a group of have-nots develops the motivation to improve their station, there are those haves or "want-to-be-haves" who are frightened by the potential competition, resent the accomplishments of those whom they view as inferior to them, or fear that this ambition is a danger to their perceived entitlement to be at the top of the social pyramid. The more success the upstarts have, the greater the resentment. Jealousy can play a big role. Eventually an incident will ignite the hatred and provide an excuse to attack and destroy. The psychological vested interest of the haves and "want-to-be-haves" is a very real threat to the interest of the have-nots. The haves are operating with a law of the jungle "kill or be killed, survival of the fittest" morality to protect themselves psychologically.

The have-nots, on the other hand, are operating on a wholly different moral level. They are not interested in taking what the haves have but are busy building their own property value, wealth, and prosperity. Their preoccupation with immediate cares makes them blind to the intensity of what they, for convenience's sake, see only as an extremely remote threat for which it is very inconvenient to give any attention to now. It is not unlike the attitude today of the middle class to the perils surrounding them: global warming, the obesity epidemic, and the coming food, water, energy, and housing insecurity. Not to mention crime and civil instability security issues.

Ignoring a problem is not a defense or a solution. Once the consequences arrive, it is too late for planning and preparations, and fate is very unforgiving. Early planning and preparation are like early detection of a terminal disease: the earlier one acts, the better the chances of survival.

When the rioting began in Tulsa, some Blacks grabbed their rifles and attempted to mount a defense. Soon bombs were dropping from airplanes, and White military personnel were shooting machine guns into the Black areas. Tulsa's Black Wall Street burned and nearly disappeared. The White citizens literally buried the matter for decades.

Destabilizing America's Middle Class

An unpleasant surprise to invisible forces interested in controlling the world's wealth was that students and activists from the wealthy American households were able to stop the war in Vietnam. The war ended in April 1975. The Federal Reserve report showing the wealth of American households at $1.7 trillion, at a time when the entire budget of the US government was $108 billion had been released in 1974.

To whatever oligarchy that has the wealth and power to affect world events, this development indicated that the American middle class had become too powerful. If their children could force the end of a war that forces in Washington, DC, had started with a trumped-up attack that never took place, on US Navy ships by North Vietnamese PT boats, what else could they do? If the students could recognize a phony premise for a war and force its end, then they may be able to recognize global warming and force an end to the use of fossil fuels or nuclear weapons or nuclear power plants. Clearly, to those who profit greatly from exerting power at the highest levels, this was unacceptable. A plan to curb the power of the middle class had to be devised and implemented in a way that would not expose those behind this attack.

Remember at the time, 1974–1975, the middle class represented the greatest concentration of wealth that had ever existed on the planet. How can they possibly be destabilized by external forces?

In analyzing how the middle class gained it wealth and influence, several factors become apparent. To remain a cohesive class, the middle class must keep growing and not become stagnant.

The key is the American dream of homeownership. From this base, the occupants mount careers, educate their children, and send them to college. These features of gainful employment, education, and property ownership are the attributes of a middle-class family and the foundation to continuing on their trajectory of upward mobility. Through education, they can enter the ranks of a learned profession, such as law, medicine, and architecture. They can become businessmen, bankers, or college professors. The most effective engine for wealth accumulation is their increasing home values. The home, through home equity loans, is a source of capital for investment and operates as an investment itself. The home, the education, the career, and many times the homeowner's business all play a role in creating and maintaining the homeowner's prosperity. Two and a half decades of growth between 1950 and 1975 created the phenomenon of the American middle class.

The entry point into the middle class and its growth potential is for a household *to form and seek homeownership.* They must have saved, have parents who will offer support, or accumulate a sufficient amount to pay what is generally 20 percent of the purchase price, a down payment. They then must have sufficient income and credit to qualify for a home mortgage. Upon surmounting these barriers, they become homeowners and are on their way to the benefits of being members of America's middle class.

If households are being formed, new homes are being constructed, purchased, and occupied; the middle class is growing and enjoying prosperity.

The middle class prospers because it has multiple paths to upward mobility. Paths include home, job, education, business, investments, and contacts. All are operating within the same time frame and simultaneously propelling upward mobility.

But what happens when the building stops? If a household cannot purchase a home, their education and employment upward mobility are negatively influenced. Without the home, the capital necessary for business and investing will generally not be available. Current employment income will not increase sufficiently to keep up the "homeowner household." The distance between renters and homeowners will begin to expand, sometimes exponentially. It will not take long for inflation to negatively impact the buying power of a household's income. New households will continue to form, but without vigorous new home construction, both home prices and rents will begin to rise. Soon, rent costs will exceed household ability to pay the rising rents. So a household has been priced out of the housing market and become homeless. The homeowner household is on its way to being the "millionaire next door." The difference is that one purchased just before construction of new affordable housing collapsed.

Now an equilibrium has set in where the only new homes being built are for the upper 25 percent or so who qualify for the expensive homes that are the only ones on the market. The builders only build for the wealthy, and only the wealthy can purchase. No one bothers with lower-cost homes because they don't sell. Willing buyers cannot qualify, and those who can qualify have more attractive options.

What happens then to the middle class is that a percentage continues upward into millionaire status and starts developing upper-class thinking. The remainder sink into working- and lower-class status. Growth stagnates. The middle class begins to disappear.

The Fortunes of the Middle Class

The middle class is closely tied to new affordable home construction. Without entry-level housing, the middle class doesn't grow, and its potential starts to die. If you want to attack and weaken the middle class, cripple the new affordable home construction capability. How? One method that has been employed is described as follows. Appeal to one of America's most powerful and widespread forces of nature, banker's greed.

The Wall Street collapse fueled by fraudulent mortgage-backed securities was brilliantly described in the film *The Big Short*. A side effect of the collapse was that affordable home building atrophied for over a decade. This caused the decline of the middle class to accelerate. The home building industry has not been able to revive its production. After being sidelined for nearly twelve years, it no longer has the logistical capability and is fighting legal and political headwinds. "Not in my backyard" (NIMBY) political opposition is now widespread. Building permits are now much more expensive and difficult to acquire. Getting to "close of escrow" and the "start of construction" is now a difficult proposition. High interest rates do not help. Qualifying for a mortgage in now more difficult. Inflation is pushing up the price of labor and materials. The more the affordable housing market atrophies, the further the decline of the middle class.

Although the source of the plan to destabilize the middle class is unknown, parts of the plan appear to have been the following:

Step 1: Use student education loans and remove or limit bankruptcy rights to saddle the students with debt to hobble them as an effective resistance. Force their best and brightest to live in a state of peonage, sometimes described as debt slavery. Cripple the capacity for protest.

Step 2: Attack the stability of the *middle-class income* by destroying middle-class jobs through automation. When cheaper options are available, ship jobs overseas. Many of the jobs shipped did not last long and ceased to exist as automation becomes available. It is estimated that 40 percent of all of today's jobs today will not exist in just a few years.

Step 3: Destabilize real estate, the foundation of their wealth, with banking excesses. Use the practice of securitization coupled with abusive bank practices described in the movie *The Big Short* whereby the banks started filling mortgage-backed securities portfolios with subprime mortgage loans that were passed off as investment-grade securities. A bubble grew and collapsed, which led to destabilization of the banking system causing high-profile investment banking firms to fail and putting commercial banks in serious jeopardy. This is what greeted the Obama administration as they took office. The collapse of the housing market coupled with banking crisis made any substantial new housing program initiatives impossible for the end of the George Bush administration and the entire Obama administration. When the Trump administration came in, Trump was proud of not advancing low-income housing to protect the housing values of existing suburban homes. The result was that the affordable home building industry was, to a great extent, shut down for about twelve years, while its capabilities atrophied.

Step 4: As the normal formation of households continues and the need for new housing grow, the home building capability is crippled. New homes that are built are prohibitively expensive. Evictions spread and grow due to higher rents while spreading homelessness.

Now the middle class and their American households are in decline. It has been destabilized and is not recovering on its own. The long-range strategy to put the middle class in its place is working, and no one has, it appears, figured out that they are under attack, let alone devised a counterattack. The obvious questions are what is the nature of the attack, who is attacking, and why? Competent adversaries will see to it that answers to these questions will never be available to their victims or their allies.

Diseases of the Middle Class

Middle-class decline is exacerbated by certain economic diseases that have affected middle-class potential. Some of these are addressed below.

1. Equilibrium in the home building market. An equilibrium is established whereby home builders adjust to market demand and build only for the prosperous who can afford their highly desirable product. Those who can no longer afford a home cannot create a demand for a product they can't afford. They are now out of the market. Whereas the homeowners are on an upward trajectory, for those without homes the trajectory is downward. This is an economic disease that causes the middle class to stop growing and go into decline. The practical effect of the banking crisis of 2008 caused this equilibrium to take hold and develop a life of its own.
2. Transformation sloth. The transformation from a self-sufficient, though difficult, work ethic lifestyle of the nineteenth-century agricultural economy into the comfort of middle-class suburban life after 1950 exposed and enabled some to adopt a lifestyle characterized by sloth, ignorance, insecurity, and opportunity for demigods. This phenomenon became visible in the second generation living in suburbia. The availability of machines like the laundry washer and dryer, the dishwasher, the refrigerator,

and a variety of other household appliances made life at home pure comfort compared to life on a farm that had no electricity or running water and where wood that had to be gathered and chopped was the primary fuel. Whereas my father was told that if you did not work to produce the food, you did not eat, the new generation felt entitled to this ease and for a breadwinner to produce a paycheck to pay for it. Along the line, there was a noticeable decline in the work ethic as this feeling of entitlement took hold. Ambitious families motivated their children to excel in school, climb the ladder of education, and create a better station for themselves. But many also enabled sloth, which was accompanied by their offspring believing that they could get way with ignorance instead of the requirement of earning an education. As it became harder to find a paycheck, insecurity would set in, coupled with resentment of those who did take advantage of education. This living in a lower station because of their ignorance coupled with its resentment of others who earned a higher station creates opportunity for demigods. I call this phenomenon transformation sloth, and I see it as an economic disease of the middle class.

3. Public education institutional stress. When education was the realm of the small schoolhouse where the teacher could concentrate on teaching the three Rs (reading, writing, and arithmetic), teachers could do a very good job of fulfilling their primary mission of teaching the fundamentals. However, when public education became big business, it also became the focus point of all the middle-class societal and family problems and less effective at education. Transformation sloth is a failure of education, both at home and in school. But it is not a simple matter. The challenges are monumental.

An insight that began to provide an appreciation for the stress our educational institutions are under was brought to my attention nearly fifty years ago and has only gotten more acute since. On our high school football team was a star player who was a very quiet person and my teammate. I signed up for a class in speed reading and was sent to the reading lab in a warehouse building that housed most of the shop classes.

Upon entering, I saw my teammate sitting next to a young lady. They were both reading the same book. We waved hi to each other as I walked past, but his face was red. Later, when the class was over, while I was walking past the table with the instructor and stopped to see the book they were reading. I was shocked to see it was a first-grade reader, *See Jane Run.* The instructor would team up a person who could read with one who could not. To my amazement, my teammate could not read and was a in his junior (eleventh grade) year. The instructor also informed me that 25 percent of the student body could not read and were in his remedial reading classes. This was a White, middle-class high school in the suburbs, an affluent area. This same school district started an accelerated honors program as a result the Russian Sputnik satellite that caused many to question the American education system.

All the problems of the American middle class end up affecting the education system. Two institutions that find themselves on the front lines, many times unfairly because the issues are not in their job description and not included in their training, are the police department and the school system. The police tend to respond with overkill, and the school district must respond with underfunded popguns. They must operate through imperfect people with their good and bad faults. Biased counselors attempted to put me, like most of their minority students, in industrial arts programs and discouraged any thought of college. They are also expected to advise those who can't read and those attempting to enter college in an equitable and professional manner. These don't even begin to shine a light of the problems facing middle-class schools. Besides gangs, violence, and drugs, political activists have attempted to polarize education. Right-wing takeover of school boards with an agenda to dictate curriculum to coincide with their beliefs is a fact of life as are the proliferation of charter schools. Those faculty and administers still trying to be educators, rather than community referees, have exhausted all avenues attempting to motivate students.

Then a person like me comes along and talks about the problems of sloth, ignorance, and loss of work ethic. Exhausted veterans greet me with a distain that I can understand. The thought that is clearly imprinted on my brain is that this is the system that will produce the leadership America must depend on throughout the twenty-first century.

Those familiar with my first treatise, published under the title *Make Luck Happen,* will not be surprised at my reaction. This is a situation that calls for citizen leadership and development of a program that will help solve the underlying issues while making most of the current barriers irrelevant. Later in this book, I will propose a program for building affordable housing for those who have currently been priced out of the market. We will continue until the real estate market is no longer dominated by a system of equilibrium. The middle class will heal through a program of building affordable housing, but now we will also include an educational and work ethic component. To the degree it is feasible, we will partner with school district and educational institutions. Despite the problems and the sloth of some, students still find motivation and leaders still emerge and go to college and climb the ladder of education.

Our program is designed to transform new middle-class households into a new and better system of self-sufficient property owners who are dependent upon the work ethic of the participant households who must learn to build their own homes and operate their small haciendas using modern labor-saving machines to achieve self-sufficiency.

How to Steal Property and Modern Land Grabs

An unfortunate assumption that you must take as gospel is bad people, who would hurt you and steal from you, do exist, and they constantly probe for weaknesses that present an opportunity to take advantage any vulnerability you inadvertently present.

An Example of Open, Blatant Theft That Occurred during Broad Daylight

An inventor worked on a machine to dispose of hazardous materials that was portable, effective, and efficient to the point that it was cost-effective.

At the time, there was nothing else on the market. He had spent years and close to $7 million in its development. One offer had come in to purchase it for $50 million. He turned it down. It was the only one in existence and there was, at that time, an urgent world need and demand.

He had a contractor's yard where he kept his equipment. The average person would not recognize anything unusual about the machine or have any idea what it was. It did not have wheels but was on skids. It weighed several tons. Then one day, when he was out of town, a truck came into his yard and picked up the machine and moved it to someone else's yard. When he went looking for it all over town, he found it and demanded its return. The owners of the yard claimed they owned the machine and that the inventor was mentally ill. It turned out that the thieves were partners with the US senator of the state who provided political connections. All officials sided with the group who now claimed ownership and the original investor was not able to prove in court that he was the owner. He never regained possession of the machine. The new owner promptly sold it to a large corporation in a foreign country for an estimated $50 million. The inventor's life's work was taken right out from under his nose because he did not take better care of its security. He was negligent in leaving it where bad people could take advantage of his lack of security and weakness.

How to Steal Real Estate

Most real estate professionals believe that recording statutes protect them. In fact, they are just another area where bad people operate, and security vigilance is both necessary and eternal.

Bad people probe for weaknesses and seize opportunities to profit from the ignorance, naivety, and negligence of good people who own, or have some rights, in real property.

Three obvious areas that I have witnessed are the following:

- the use of forgeries. A bad actor will pay to obtain a convincing but fake driver's license and have a notary acknowledge the signature on a deed where he conveys property owned by someone else that he is impersonating to a third party. The third party then borrows a substantial amount of money on this property that was supposed to have sold to him by the real owner. Because the property was worth over $700,000 and held free and clear, the borrower, the alleged owner, receives $400,000 in loan proceeds, which he splits with ID thief, and they leave town. The lender forecloses on the property. If no one is taking care of the property and the original owner gets no notice, the property is gone to the lender who acted in good faith. Title insurance may or may not catch it.

- use of liens. Many times, a property with equity will become the subject of liens, such as mortgages, tax liens, judgments, HOA liens, mechanic's liens, and prescriptive rights, and an informed person may want the property. An unscrupulous operator may buy the lien and use it to illegally foreclose on the property by using physical and legal means to prevent the real owner from receiving notice of default and notice of auction and be there to take the land at a very low price. The real owner has lost the property and doesn't even know it.

- occupancies in violation of law and the prescriptive rights of adverse possession. If a person moves on your land that no one is attending to and lives there like it is his or her own and, in California, pays the taxes on it, after five years, the statute of limitations to evict him expires and he is effectively the owner of the land by adverse possession because no one kicked him off in time.

These are among the opportunities presented to bad actors by an owner's prolonged absence from, or inattention to, the property. Are these only the tip of the iceberg? Be an attentive owner.

How to Buy a Home

The best way to buy a home is ask a local licensed Realtor to represent you in searching for a home. They know the local market and the legal requirements set up to protect the innocent from bad actors. To stay in business, they also must know how to get their deals financed. They know the territory and the local ins and outs. If they don't succeed in closing a deal for you, they don't get paid.

How did America's middle class build the wealth of American households described in the 1974 Federal Reserve report?

Four factors enabled the post-World War II creation of middle-class real estate wealth:

1. mortgage loan origination infrastructure through savings and loan associations, commercial banks, credit unions, private mortgage companies, government agencies, and other loan originators supported by secondary market structures
2. mass employment with high-paying wages, driven by unions, that enabled payment of the debt service needed to support the mortgage loans created by market demand
3. construction infrastructure capability to produce homes to satisfy demand
4. a supportive public policy whereby government encouraged growth, especially of the tax base

The Roosevelt New Deal administrations enabled creation of a secondary market to purchase what were considered risky amortized loans made to working-class borrowers by mortgage loan originators. These were loans guaranteed by the Federal Housing Administration (FHA). The organization that purchased these loans was the Federal National Mortgage Association (Fannie Mae). It would bundle them into packages composed of hundreds of millions of dollars in loans. These bundles were then auctioned on Wall Street to long-term investors. I once meet the person in charge of investing the monthly premiums paid to a major life insurance company. He said his job was to responsibly invest over $600 million a month. The ability to purchase government-guaranteed bundles in packages of $300 million each at one time made his job easier. The large institutional investors populate Wall Street and are always looking for large, safe investments.

In time, the good experience with low default rates and the restrictions placed by the government to prevent government-guaranteed loans being made to high-income borrowers who did not need the help led to the creation of the Federal Home Loan Mortgage Corporation (Freddie Mac) to enable a secondary market for conventional nonguaranteed loans. The private and government-guaranteed loans turned out to be among the safest of investments. As a result, financing has always been available to qualified American home buyers.

With the creation of viable secondary market to purchase, aggregate, and sell at auction large numbers of loans, a vehicle and market was established for loan originators. With the housing demand created by veterans returning from World War II, states like California started approving a significant number of charters for new savings and loan associations to originate mortgage loans. If a savings and loan took in $100,000 in deposits, it could make ten $10,000 home loans and charge 1 percent in origination fees. That is $1,000 in profit. When the $100,000 was gone, they could then sell the loans to the secondary market and get their $100,000 back to make ten more loans. They would also agree to service the loan by collecting the monthly payments and sending them to the secondary lender for another 1 percent or so fee from the payment amount. If they could make ten loans a month, collect the fees, and sell them to the secondary market and take in another $100,000 in deposits a month, their growth and income turn them into moneymaking machines. They started recruiting builders and offering construction financing to them to build and sell homes. A huge infrastructure grew up of building contractors and financing institutions that worked to satisfy the needs of the American households that were forming and needed housing. The modern suburbs movement took root and grew. By 1974, American households would represent the greatest concentration of wealth that has ever existed in the history of the planet.

None of this would have been possible without the economic growth that occurred after World War II. Factories and workers were needed to build cars, home appliances, farm equipment, airplanes, homes, and all the other goods and services demanded by the prospering Americans whose surplus income drove the postwar economy. Unions grew and kept wages growing at a rate commensurate with economic growth and profit. These wages provided the debt service to make the payments on the mortgage loans.

The unsung heroes of this growth were the small builders who used to build most homes. When Kaufman and Board was the largest home builder in the country, it only built 1 percent of the total. The small builder client of a savings and loan was a major factor in building affordable housing. Generally, if a builder could secure a building site free and clear of loans, construction financing was assured. It was the large builders who got the attention and business of wealthy clients, but the large number of small builders drove the high production numbers.

Equilibrium Issues Stifles Affordable Housing Production

California coastal housing market has reached, and the remainder of the state is trending to follow, an equilibrium. Developers build for the market that can qualify to pay for at least the median home costs. In a county like Los Angeles, the median home costs are well over $700,000. These higher-income markets generate greater profits and provide a dependable market for lenders and builders.

The situation in the state is rapidly reaching an equilibrium like that found in areas of the Central Valley like Tulare County. There is a vibrant housing market in Tulare County for the economically affluent White population who can afford their median housing price. Those outside this demographic do not fit into the market equilibrium and are ignored because they cannot afford to purchase the homes being built to serve this market. Sixty-two percent of the county is now Hispanic. Many of them fit into two classifications: the low income and what is referred to as the very low income. This population is priced out this local market, which has reached a comfortable equilibrium without them. The low- and very low-income percentage of the population has risen since it first came to my attention, and it has continued to rise. It is virtually impossible to find anyone to undertake the challenge of developing housing for this low-income demographic when governmental financing is not available. As a result, 62 percent of the population is without even the prospect of affordable housing.

This trend has migrated to the expensive housing markets located in the coastal areas of the state. The fate of the underserved class of Tulare County reflects the growing predicament of a huge percentage of California's middle class.

Unless you can accumulate a 20 percent a down payment and have a household income well over $100,000 a year to qualify for a mortgage, you are already priced out of the housing market in Los Angeles County, where the median home price is now about $800,000. The median household income is $68,000, just about half the income needed to qualify. Over half of the households in Los Angeles County now share a fate like the poor of Tulare County when it comes to the American dream of homeownership. This is a symptom and example of the evaporating middle class in California.

America's Evaporating Middle Class Needs Help

As described above at page 32 in the section on destabilizing the middle class, the institutions that have supported both the American middle class and its working class are evaporating. Most Americans have believed they were protected by a vibrant economy, strong job markets, options for affordable housing, and many pathways to earn an education. Despite a propensity for complaining, they had confidence in a competent, responsive government that could cope with society's challenges.

Over recent decades, however, it has become increasingly apparent that this security appears to be evaporating.

Perils That Many in the Middle Class May Not Recognize but Soon Will Be Forced to Confront

1. Wildfires. As a young person in the 1950s in Southern California, we would see news of forest fires. Large wildfires were seldom in the city or suburbs. Today, with a great assist from global warming, wildfires strike anywhere in the state. We now witness the spectacle of burning embers being blown by high winds into the eaves of wood-frame homes and causing them to burn quickly like tinderboxes and setting off a firestorm that devours entire subdivisions. We have now seen thousands of extremely expensive homes burn like kindling. Middle-class homes are no longer the

supersafe bastions of security. They can now go up in smoke at any time.

2. Bad weather and insurance. Portions of the Gulf Coast, where the place of oil in the economy causes many inhabitants to favor oil company's interests politically, are becoming victims. They tend to be very protective of the petroleum industry. Now the frequency of storms and the damage they bring have caused insurance companies to stop issuing policies. Those who are remaining in business are having to increase premiums so high that it may become impossible for many current inhabitants to continue living there. They supported the oil companies, but now they may have nowhere to go.

3. The electricity grid. The grid is aging and vulnerable. Fossil fuels are the cheapest source of electricity but contribute to global warming. It is not clear that renewable sources of energy will be able to displace fossil fuels. Electromagnetic pulse attacks could disable the grid. Hostile nations and terrorists have an inviting vulnerable target that can cause real pain to the American middle class.

4. Water insecurity is apparent if Flint, Michigan, and Jackson, Mississippi. California frequently experiences global warming-influenced droughts. This is only the beginning.

5. Housing for children of middle-class families. Only 25 percent of potential home buyers can afford to buy a home in Southern California. The median price is near $800,000, and the median income is about $56,000. Seventy-five percent of the population are priced out of the market. The children of middle-class families will expect homes of their own. Unless the housing crisis is successfully resolved soon, housing for this group may be lost permanently. The American dream may turn into the American mirage.

6. Working poor homelessness. As more and more of the working poor are evicted and forced into homelessness, the housing crisis will worsen and the plight of the poor will continue to deteriorate.

7. Food insecurity and supply. Fifty percent of the food consumed in the United States is grown in California's Central Valley. The labor force responsible for this harvest is primarily immigrants

and undocumented workers from Latin America. During the pandemic, there was concern that if the workforce starts dying off, the crops America depends on will be wiped out and ignite a food crisis. Some irresponsible Republican politicians have persecuted these people. They have accused them of taking Americans' jobs, of being criminals, rapist, and drug dealers. Most of the undocumented that I know are hardworking, honest people who do backbreaking work in very difficult conditions for salaries in the range of $20,000 a year. Their children were hurt and incredulous to hear the president of the United States telling such mean lies about their parents. But anti-immigrant groups loved it, and they are who President Trump was playing up to. Untrue, defamatory, and misleading allegations like this cause incalculable lasting harm far beyond the immediate audience.

8. Drug use, addiction, and gun violence. Drug cartels could not prosper or exist without two made-in-America items. First, America provides the market that pays for the products marketed by the cartels. The cartels and local drug pushers sell death, and Americans, more and more, buy and pay for it. And second, America is home to the greatest and largest arms dealers in the world. Guns from America give the cartels their firepower and destabilize minority communities where the drug culture is entrenched. Just like the concerns generated by the war in Vietnam being stopped by the middle-class students, the successes of the civil rights movement were evidence that the Black civil rights infrastructure had to be destabilized. Soon crack cocaine flooded the ghettos along with guns. Gun purveyors skillfully hide behind the Second Amendment to the US Constitution to prevent gun control. Drug deaths everywhere and gun deaths in minority neighborhoods are off the charts and appear to be out of control.

The most effective weapon is to take the profit out of the activity, and it will die. The history of more and more stringent "get tough" laws and progressively more draconian punishments have proven ineffective over the past fifty years unless used for political advantage of some politicians. If you only want a political issue, keep things as they are. When you really want to deal with the problem, take the profit out of it. The easiest way to do this is legalize the drugs and have the state regulate them. If you can get the drug free at a place where the option of treatment is also available, there is no reason to pay for it and give business to the local drug pushers and their cartel bosses. If their market dries up, they dry up. If they have no money for ammunitions and guns, guns become impractical and counterproductive.

The Role of Misinformation, Propaganda, and Sophistry

There are various special interest groups who have a stake in making and keeping the American people, especially the middle class, divided. The divisions prevent the middle class from collectively recognizing that they have a joint problem and taking united action to solve it. This is critical to the special interest if the obvious solution may be detrimental to the special interest group. An example would be recognition of the dangers of global warming to the middle class and the acceptance that the solution is to switch to other sources of energy. If the American people can be divided, and remain divided, they will not unite to force change. Some very talented people have been paid millions to use sophistry, propaganda, and misinformation to see that no change will take place. A major supplier of such funds has been the Koch brothers, who control petroleum product pipelines, and Exxon Mobile Corporation, whose lifeblood is fossil fuel.

When government does not work, citizens must demonstrate leadership. Those competent to do so must take the initiative and confront the challenges we collectively face.

There is a severe shortage of affordable housing units in California today, and it is destroying a key support for middle-class families. Homelessness has descended upon California's major cities like a plague and is tearing away at the fabric of municipal life. As rental housing costs rise beyond the income of a working family to pay, the workforce is forced into homelessness. There they join the mentally afflicted, the drug addicts, the underclass, and other dysfunctional poor. Once here, the environment is rife with unfortunates competing for meager resources that are necessary to their survival. The road out gets steeper and steeper until escape requires so enormous an effort that the available resources cannot provide, and escape becomes virtually impossible.

The middle class needs to renew itself and be better. It needs to resurrect a strong and healthy affordable home building program. This program needs to include the availability of alternate infrastructure as a reserve for the coming failures of the main systems as we confront the reality and coming legacy of global warming, our inheritance from the petroleum industry. It needs to be stronger, renew its wealth growth, and increase its capability to defend itself against the forces of division and stealth attacks.

How can the economic casualties who are now refugees of the economic system regain control of their destiny? Given the circumstances, what can a private citizen do to alleviate the suffering and provide these economic casualties a path to a more productive existence?

If concerned citizens have, or are willing to learn, the skills to develop a methodology for solving these issues and are also willing to undertake the enormous effort required for success, then the answer is *plenty*.

Fundamentally, it is an issue of competence. The issue with competence is that those who can, generally will not, and those who will, generally cannot because they don't know how. The motivation for professionals with expertise is that they expect to be paid handsomely for their services, and they have no desire to work extraordinarily hard to solve exceedingly difficult problems where they may face failure. They have no intentions of putting forth the sacrifice necessary to solve the housing problems of the working poor homeless population. Those that are willing to sacrifice and accept responsibility for their neighbors do not have the skills or wealth to make it happen. Nevertheless, many try to do what they can. These efforts should be supported.

One advocate for developing transformative skills is Rico Vidas. He has made a career of developing expertise for doing good and being a good citizen to his community. Rico Vidas authored and published a book called *Make Luck Happen*. The book describes and advocates leadership by private individuals to solve public issues using the problem-solving protocols described in the book. Here are his recommendations for a solution.

Issues to Be Addressed to Resolve the Housing Crisis in California

The crisis goes beyond affordability. These include the following:

a. Thousands of housing units have literally burned up. For the last century, builders in California have relied on wood-frame construction technology. This material makes homes vulnerable to powerful wildfires, many driven by strong winds that appear to be a result of climate change.

b. Municipal NIMBY ("not in my backyard") regulations present barriers to the issuance of building permits. These have prevented the construction of low-income and affordable housing. Whereas "expensive" building permits in the 1970s would generally cost less than $2,000, a building permit in San Diego today can require about $60,000. Land costs have risen as the values of homes have increased. Before new home construction can even start, the builder may be required to pay $60,000 in permits plus hundreds of thousands of dollars in land costs, and then another $25,000 and/or more must be paid in architectural and engineering fees. It is now becoming standard to pay up front for the right to build almost as much as the entire costs of an affordable home. The result is effectively doubling the housing costs. In Los Angeles County and throughout Southern California, the total cost to acquire a permit can run well over $15,000 and include fees for schools and other municipal expenses.

This was compounded by President Trump when he bragged that he has saved suburban property values by denying funding for low-income housing. Whereas in past administrations, evidence of a housing shortages would spur HUD to provide incentives and financing for low-income and moderate-income housing, during the Trump administration, this federal housing agency was not engaged, greatly adding to the housing shortage and increasing the cost of new housing. This may change under new administrations, but it takes time to gear up and initiate action that produces results. This assumes that both the major parties in Congress cooperate with funding. This is not at all assured.

The California Legislature has passed dozens of laws to combat barriers created by municipal regulations, but there is one area where the state has no jurisdiction. The state cannot rescind or amend the law of supply and demand. Substantially increasing the number of housing units can positively influence the crisis in a positive manner *if* it is characterized by a substantial increase in affordability. This is the issue we intend to solve.

c. With the supply of building sites shrinking, there is need for creative nontraditional housing developers who can find and secure land and navigate past the barriers to housing development.

The Emergence of Solutions

Rico Vidas has studied the problem and believes that there is a solution that can be implemented by ordinary citizens if there is qualified, competent leadership.

We are told by responsible mortgage bankers that if the home costs of a three-bedroom, two-bath home were in the range of half the median costs and the qualifying household annual income was nearer to half the median income, then there would be a large supply of qualified buyers, not only in Los Angeles County but throughout Southern California.

There used to be two main costs that drove up home prices. These were high union labor costs and the high costs for materials. Land costs could be held to 20 percent of the home's value, and professional fees and permit costs were less than 5 percent. Now front-end professional fees and permit charges have become a major factor, and high costs of new homes have driven up land costs.

Labor and material costs have now been joined by land costs and government fees to provide a full range of financial and logistical barriers to affordable housing in California. The current housing crisis bears witness to how effective these barriers have been.

This is good news because it lays out the challenge and defines the problem to be solved. As set forth in Rico Vidas's book *Make Luck Happen,* the following steps set forth the protocols of problem-solving to be applied to this crisis:

Step 1 to problem-solving is problem recognition and definition. At first blush, it appears that all we have to do is find a developer who can dream up ways to either cope with or lower costs, be they labor, material, professional, and/or government fees and costs.

Step 2 is information gathering, which always turns out to be an ongoing process full of surprises, generally of the unpleasant variety.

Step 3 is analysis of the information.

Step 4 is formulation of goals. This requires making value decisions and establishing priorities.

Step 5 is strategy. The implications arising from your analysis and goals will suggest your strategy.

Step 6 is implementation of your strategy.

Step 7 is feedback and evaluation. This is the ongoing information gathering. Now your information includes the experience gained from your efforts at implementation.

Step 8 is reformulation of goals using new information gained by experience. You now start over with a sophisticated version of trial and error until the problem is solved.

Analysis, Goals, and Strategy

The analysis defines the problems in four sets of costs. Labor and material costs joined by land costs and front-end soft costs necessary to obtain a building permit. The implication is that affordability will follow if these costs can be lowered or managed.

Experience suggests, however, that additional steps may be needed to succeed in reaching these stated goals. Financing plays a crucial role. Mortgage funds may be available, but the underwriting credit criteria may bar financing for those in greatest need.

The solution is to lower the costs of housing and to solve any financial, legal, and/or surprise barriers that may appear.

The questions become these: How do you lower construction costs, land costs, and construction permit processing costs? How do you deal with financing barriers? How do you plan for barriers that are currently unforeseen?

Using experience as a banker, contractor, and developer, the following strategy is set forth to accomplish these goals.

Initial Strategy

1. Lower construction materials costs. Find a way to fabricate building materials that are better suited and less expensive for construction. Given the wildfire potential, a switch to steel-reinforced concrete block to today's reality, driven by global warming. Concrete block construction is resistant to tornadoes, hurricanes, earthquakes, and wildfires. Today the cost is prohibitive, but new technologies we have developed will substantially lower the cost to about a third of wood-frame construction. We cannot affect lumber prices the way we can affect the price of concrete blocks. Adobe homes are still in use in the United States after five hundred years. Concrete may be what we need to deal with global warming. We are confident that we will be able to use steel-reinforced concrete masonry units as our primary building material at a fraction of the costs of wood-frame construction. How we decide to structure the program is a work in progress.

2. Lower labor costs. We have a license to use an interlocking concrete block building system that requires no mortor and does not require skilled labor masons. Using the system, trained laborers can triple the output of skilled masons using conventional methods. This system uses interlocking blocks to allow nonskilled labor to set the blocks. We will use one design over and over. We will design for simplicity and ease of installation. We will have experts design plumbing kits and electrical kits for rapid assembly and train persons to become specialists at their installation. That will be the only tasks they do. We will become expert at rapid installation. Owner builders can participate. We have plans for systems of labor barter. We are confident that we cut labor costs substantially.

3. Professional fees. Using new technology and old tactics, we greatly reduce these costs. Architects who will work for lower fees are available using web sites like freelancers where these professionals

must bid against each other for the job. Competition is a great regulator against price gouging.

A tactic we have used in prior years is to create one set of plans and use them over and over. The architect only must adjust to the terrain of the current site. The bulk of the plan drawings and specifications are reused at a fraction of the costs.

4. We believe that by using the strategies mentioned above, we can eliminate about two-thirds of the cost of construction.

5. Land costs. There are many strategies for securing land by negotiating lower prices. Sometimes a few may work. Higher home prices invariably lead to higher land price expectations in the minds of landowners.

Cash, financing incentives, joint ventures, or pursuing undeveloped raw acreage will be the strategies we pursue to lower land costs.

Cash. Money talks and we intend to work hard maintaining liquidity that will support credibility while making cash offers. Cash offers are always below what we perceive as market value. If the owner wants the entire asking price up front, then we want a cash discount.

Financing Incentives

I will pay your full asking price if you give me site control now so that I can obtain a building permit that allows me to secure a construction loan and pay for the land, not with my cash but with loan proceeds. I will pay more for assistance with my financing costs and my liquidity.

Joint Ventures

Let's be partners. You put up the land, and we do the rest. Afterward, we sell for cash, we get back our construction costs, and then we split the rest.

Raw Acreage

Urban land is expensive because the municipality has installed sewer lines, utility lines, and convenience services and has provided a more reliable market. If you build on raw acreage, these services typically do not exist. The developer must install them. It can become awfully expensive to install electrical, water, and sewer lines from the current utility lines to your location. Zoning requirements to install paved roads, curbs, and sidewalks can present expensive barriers.

Raw acreage can generally be secured at lower prices because of the barriers to developing it. Many times, when you reduce the present land value by these infrastructure costs, the land will have little or no value.

We see this as an opportunity to develop our Cal Hacienda Independent Estates where we incorporate self-sufficient capability. We have found technologies to provide water, electricity, food, sanitation, communications, and transportation on land that no one would want because of the difficulties to develop it. We can do this affordably and provide housing to those in severe need and without other options.

How to Build a One-to-Four Unit Residential Project When You Have Insufficient Cash and Are Starting from Scratch

A lesson I learned doing large projects was that if you can close a construction loan, then a project can be built, qualify for permanent financing, and provide an asset that can be rented or sold. I got very good at finding a building site and carrying the project to closing of the construction loan. I reasoned that if I could find a way to do for large projects, then I should be able to find a way for a single home.

This is how I am attempting to jump-start coming out of retirement and successfully confronting California's current housing crisis.

The primary requirement for a construction loan is a building permit. A building permit requires plans and specifications prepared by architects and engineers that can be reviewed and approved by a municipality's central permit bureau. The owner of the property must authorize the submission of the request for building permit. The desired use must be approved by the planning commission. The real estate developer is confronted with the initial barriers to overcome. Funds to buy the land or to establish site control with an option or contract. Funds to pay engineers and architects to produce the plans and specifications. After review and approval, the permit fees must be paid. There is the review fee, but now these fees have become a revenue source. Fees must also now be paid to the local school district and various municipal agencies. Generally, this is not an insignificant amount. In fact, it can be a real barrier to come up with substantial funds after having paid the various professional fees, the initial land costs, and negotiations with building contractors and sometime key suppliers. Paying these costs is what seed money is all about. Today, the state of California offers, within budgetary limits, a grant of up to $40,000 to homeowners to pay seed money costs of installing an ADU (accessory dwelling unit) on their property.

My strategy is to divide the various elements to secure a building permit in manageable elements that I can accomplish piecemeal. I know that if I can complete one home, it will be a template for others. I divided the various elements into smaller, less expensive units so that I can make incremental progress and negotiate as much as possible along the way. I purchased inexpensive land upon which I could install off-grid infrastructure. If I can get to construction loan closing, the infrastructure could be paid for out of the loan proceeds rather than from up front seed money. Rather than paying $400,000 for land in Pasadena, I bought desert land for $6,000 that I could finance with a small pension. An architect from the company licensing the interlocking brick technology prepared a generic design for a four-bedroom, two-bath home that will have local professionals assist me to complete for submission for a building permit. Using the generic design, I am shopping for the materials, appliances, and fixtures that will be installed. I want to have a handle on costs and independently be able to supply these items. These will also be listed in our specifications to assist during the plan review phase of the permit application.

Upon issuance of the building permit, I will negotiate with a general contractor who can provide both a payment and a performance bond. I will find and prequalify financing for a purchaser for the project. With a purchaser for the finished product, a contractor's bond to guarantee that the project will be built, and a building permit to commence construction, I am in position to apply for a construction loan. The way the project is structured, nearly all risks have been hedged. A construction loan should be a simple matter. The sale of the first project will produce sufficient seed funds for a second home project. With the sale of the first home, we will then be underway with our program.

A plan for securing a building permit that includes the following was necessary:

- architect and engineer solutions
- building site options
- funds for building permit fees
- contractor's performance and payment bonds.
- prequalified purchaser at completion of construction

With these in hand, a construction loan becomes feasible.

Upon completion of construction, the sales proceeds will kick off the long-range program for home construction in California.

Subdivisions

If you wish to develop five or more homes on a single parcel, you need to comply with both the Subdivision Map Act and the Subdivided Lands Act. The Map Act is prepared by a surveyor who draws an outline of the parcel and divides it into individual parcels on paper. This subdivision map must be approved by the local planning authority and either the city council or county board of supervisors. A condominium is a vertical subdivision. Once approved, the individual units can be legally conveyed, provided there is compliance with the Subdivided Lands Act. Unlike the Map Act, this is a consumer protection law designed to give a buyer accurate and full disclosure of all issues concerning the property. No lot can be sold until a prospective buyer has signed a receipt of the Subdivision Report White Paper, a report prepared by the California Department of Real Estate, three days before the sale. After the application for this report, the processing period is seldom less than nine months.

The Problem with Mortgages and New Approaches to Homeownership

Sources of debt service have become unstable. A stable employment base is necessary to a stable marketplace. The old idea of saving up for a home while you live in the house now leads to a lot of foreclosures. Whereas in the 1950s a good job generally meant an income for thirty years to pay off the mortgage, now it appears we will have at least one or two nationwide economic catastrophes in that timeline whereby incomes disappear. Will there be sufficient time to amortize the loan?

Today, a mortgage is not as safe as it would seem. A borrower doesn't know whether there will be stable income for thirty years. Now the idea should be how to pay off your mortgage as soon as possible. The process can be speeded up by paying extra principal payments in the early days of amortization. Also, look for investments that provide returns that make large payments toward payoff. Concentrate on paying off the mortgage loan while you still have time.

Cal Hacienda Lifestyle Center for Self-Sufficient Livings and Alternative Infrastructure Skills

A new group of ladies and gentlemen will be accepted to participate in an education and training programs and, upon graduation, become members of the Cal Hacienda Society of Independent Self-Sufficient Property Owners who are trained in self-sufficient living and can excel as survival warriors.

They will be distinguished for having been trained by Cal Hacienda in self-sufficiency and have achieved a related set of learned skills designed to enable an independent and self-sufficient lifestyle.

All graduates will have the skills as to how to build their own home, secure water, generate electricity, arrange home sanitation, provide communications, enable travel by electric vehicles, and grow enough food. They will also learn how to finance the purchase of the equipment required and how to use their newly developed assets to create sources of income.

These skills will include, among others, the following:

1. Skills for securing water from four different sources, separate and apart from municipal utility districts. These will include skills in the following:
    A. Distilling seawater and other brackish water into fresh, distilled water.
    B. Use of dehumidifiers to extract water from the air we breathe and the atmosphere around us.
    C. Rainwater capture and storage, including navigating the legal minefield encountered in many jurisdictions.
    D. Drilling water wells in both aquifer and primary water reservoirs.
        *   *Aquifer* refers to underground reservoirs created by rainwater seepage underground.
        *   *Primary water* refers to water created by friction between underground plates and forces that cause hydrogen and oxygen to be pressed together at great pressure, resulting in the formation of water reservoirs deep underground.
2. The generation of electricity using on-site and off-grid solar panels and portable generators.
    A. These generators will use internal combustion engines converted and adapted to use gasoline, propane, digester biogas, and hydrogen electrolyzed from water.
    B. When available, Metrol, a diesel substitute, will be introduced. All electricity will be stored in batteries, using modern technology, but also using Edison batteries from the turn of the nineteenth century, which have a rated life of sixty-five years.
3. Transportation using the following:
    A. Electric bicycles that can carry extra batteries and pull small trailers.
    B. Electric automobiles.
    C. Existing vehicles modified to enable their internal combustion engines (ICEs) to be fueled and powered by hydrogen, natural gas, digester biogas, producer gas (which powered Australia during World War II), and/or Metrol when available. All will be equipped with adapter technology enabling them to use these alternate fuels.

4. Communications using satellite internet to enable streaming television and smartphone technologies. If, and when, those become disabled for whatever reasons, we will still be able to communicate because we have, and know how to use, walkie-talkies, licenses that allow us to use ham radios, flag signals when necessary, and finally, Morse code communicated by reflecting mirrors by day and flashlights by night.

5. Food production using hothouse permaculture technology, freight-food automated food-growing containers, experimental hydroponic pocket farms, and the traditional victory gardens. During World War II, 60 percent of Americans produced their own food through victory gardens. A popular World War I poster featured a female angel dressed like a soldier sowing seeds over plowed ground with the caption reading, "Every Garden a Munitions Plant."

Why Our Youth Need the Opportunity to Benefit from the Programs Proposed in This Treatise

A realistic look at the paths available today upon graduation from high school. Options include the following:

1. Enter the workforce and take your chances on the economy. Look for a job that both pays well and has a future. Often that means settling for whatever you can get to pay the rent, purchase gas or bus fare, and put food on the table. You are gambling on the economy and whatever opportunities and rewards it will provide. Without education, connections, or a learned trade, such as a plumber and electrician, the prospects are very high that you will be condemned to a life of economic insecurity living paycheck to paycheck with constantly rising rents and an inability to get ahead financially. The proverbial rat race. In old age, you will have to survive as best you can on a small social security pension.

The Corporate Option

There is also the case of the high school graduates and college graduates who believe that they have been very fortunate to have been hired by a large corporation. They were among the bright ones in their class and now enjoy the security of a large, seemingly well-financed institution. There is the potential for upward mobility, pension, medical benefits, and whatever perks they can negotiate. They marry, buy a home generally using two incomes to qualify, and life is good. A prosperous future seems assured. Children are on the way, and the family's foundation is well established.

The first and second child arrive, and the costs and strains of parenting, not to mention day care, become chronic issues. And as they are adjusting to this new reality, news hits that the corporation they work for has announced layoffs due to a downturn in the overall economy or that the number of jobs will soon be cut in half due to a merger with another corporation to cut costs. Whatever a person's job is in their present company, that same job is being performed in the merging company. What is now two jobs will soon become one job, and only one of the two employees will be hired by the new surviving company. About 50 percent of the workforce will be gone, and they find that chances are good that they will lose their job.

These decisions are made by greedy bankers who are in control at the highest levels. Employees have little say in the decision-making process. I am familiar with a case of a woman who found herself in a merger after working for twenty years. She was forty-seven and the young woman in the other company doing her job was twenty-four with a lower salary. They kept the twenty-four-year-old and laid off the forty-seven-year-old. The forty-seven-year-old soon discovered that at her age, she was now unemployable. Whereas at twenty-four, she never had a problem, at forty-seven no one wanted to hire her. Employees of large corporations are pawns to senior management and their bankers. Their sense of security was merely a mirage projected by their inexperience and youthful desires. Now what do they do? Most look for another job. Occasionally they find one that pays much less than they were used to. For the others, the potential for homelessness and an all-consuming struggle just to survive becomes real.

2. Enroll in an academic institution if you can afford it. A college education is a wonderful thing. The academic rigor of having to learn your history and know how you came to be in America in the twenty-first century along with the fundamentals of science and the arts changes a student for the better. Middle-class competency for leadership and achievement is born here. I remember a lecture on the nature of different social classes. A fundamental point that the speaker emphasized was that members of a lower class cannot tell the difference between themselves and members of an upper class. But members of the upper class can see a clear difference. A college education pushes its participants solidly into the middle class. When you interact with two high school graduates after one has graduated from college and the other went straight into the workforce, you can tell the difference between them. The college education shows. The potential for success, leadership, and accomplishment is clearly visible as are the limitations in potential for the high school graduate.

Whereas the value of a college education is obvious in terms of quality of life regardless of questions of income, how to finance an educational experience has become increasingly problematic.

For as long as I can remember, available scholarships awarded based on merit provided the funds for qualified students to finance their education. Loans play only a small role. Overall, a qualified student who really wanted to go to college could, with effort, find entrance and financial support to get into college. Generally, if they made it through the first year, they would be savvy enough to complete their education through a combination of scholarships and part time employment.

The Student Loan Trap

Initially it appeared that government-guaranteed loan programs were good for the middle class. Now my view is that hidden within the programs' structure was a trap for the middle class that is just now becoming apparent. Before describing the trap, we must understand a few features of the state law and constitutional law concerning the relationship between creditors and debtors in America. Specifically, the law on predatory loans and an examination of why student loans can be difficult to discharge in bankruptcy.

Predatory loans, in addition to including a host of unconscionable terms, conditions, fees, interest, and costs, may have as a key factor loans that are made to borrowers who cannot reasonably pay them back. In California, if all the elements are present, it can be a crime to make a loan to a borrower who you know cannot pay it back. There is a section in the constitution that authorizes Congress to enact uniform laws about bankruptcies. This is not a citizen's constitutional right to bankruptcy but a grant of power to Congress to enact whatever laws it deems appropriate about bankruptcy. Hence, student loan legislation can be enacted under whatever terms Congress deems appropriate, including exempting student loans from bankruptcy. At the time this legislation was passed, many legislators expressed concerns that students would take out loans, then upon graduation, filing bankruptcy to avoid paying the loan. This was the reason given for the inclusion of student loans among those debts that were not dischargeable in bankruptcy.

The practical effect was that loans were made to students who had no guaranteed ability to repay them but who, along with Congress, were gambling that after their education was completed, they would be able to earn sufficient funds to repay the loan. The difference is that if the student is simply unable to pay, he is rendered into a state of debt peonage with his life overwhelmed and controlled by debt. If the student cannot demonstrate substantial hardship and pay the attorneys and other legal costs of an adversary proceeding in bankruptcy, he is trapped in debt for at least twenty years. This generally means that the student will also not be able to qualify to purchase a home. It amounts to twenty years of struggle without the ability to advance in life and will never reach the potential that student loans were supposed to enable. As things have worked out, the financial bubbles, recessions, technological disruptions, automation, market crashes, globalization, and general economic instability have changed the landscape for stable employment, and many assumptions Congress made have proved inaccurate.

A generation of Americans has had the American dream deliberately placed beyond their reach by forces that enticed them to take out student loans that were beyond their ability to pay comfortably and which disqualified them from building wealth through homeownership.

The two previous generations of America's middle-class students were the shock troops in the civil rights movement and protesting the war in Vietnam and played a major role forcing an end to the war. The middle class, it would appear, was so powerful through the combination of its wealth and student activists that it was able to force an end to a war that was not in its interest but very much in the interest of the military-industrial complex and their bankers who profit enormously from war. If the middle class was that powerful, potentially they could force a change from fossil fuels to clean energy or any other practices that are not in their interest but very profitable to anonymous groups with conflicting interest.

It is in the interest of these anonymous groups to find ways to disrupts the forces, events, and assets that extend the power of the middle class, but in an anonymous manner. This may very well explain the reasons for the decline of the middle class.

Is it possible that well-financed think tanks were paid to come up with a plan of action to disrupt the power of the middle class? The combination of student loans that hobbled student activists and the damage to the housing market brought about by the massive fraud engaged in by bankers selling mortgage-backed securities that had the ancillary effect of pricing a large and growing portion of the middle class out of the housing market. The market is difficult and is about to get far worse for first-time buyers and the lower half of the middle class. In Southern California, 75 percent of the home buying market can no longer qualify for a home mortgage or afford the down payment. The percentage of the middle class who own homes is shrinking and is about to get a lot worse.

3. Enroll in a technical education and learn a trade or industrial skill. Again, you are gambling on the economy. You are also gambling on your ability to enter a program through the union controlling the trade. There are only a limited number of positions that open periodically. Will your function be automated and make your trade skills obsolete? How long will your exceptional trade income hold up?

4. Enter Cal Hacienda's Self-Sufficient Lifestyle Education and Training Program, and use your newly acquired assets to pursue an academic degree. When the degree is awarded, an available option is to apply to professional school to enter a learned profession, such as medicine, law, engineering, and architecture. Upon completion, because you own an income-producing Cal Hacienda Estate, you have the freedom and ability to do anything you desire.

End-Game Goals

1. Student loans have been replaced by scholarship grants and a functioning path to homeownership in place for low-income home buyers.

2. New sources of income, new sources of food, and internet businesses are in place.

3. Homes are being produced, some without mortgages, along with powerful new wealth programs, and the middle class has started growing again.

4. The middle class is again characterized by a healthy housing market satisfying the needs of newly formed households.

PART 2

"LESSONS OF NATURE" USING VIRUS TACTICS FOR FINANCE

There appear to be these two well-defined paths toward major financial success in America:

- path 1: leverage and banking
- path 2: the five elements solution

Financial leverage uses a small amount of money to move and invest large sums of money. The qualifying as small amounts can be

- seed money from friends and family
- initial capital from a private placement
- bank or SBA Loans
- venture capital, private equity, and angel investors

With launch of the business accomplished with small amounts, large amounts can come from the following:

- investment bankers and an *initial public offering*
- investment bankers and *debt financing*
- *home mortgage loans:* Most mortgages make use of leverage. A 20 percent down payment enables an 80 percent loan. The mortgage industry is built on leverage.
- *leveraged buyouts:* These are described above in the example on LBOs. Now that you have regained private ownership of your debt-laden business, how long and how much did it cost? Projections are about thirty years to be debt free and millions of dollars in fees and interest.

Path 2: Implement the Five Elements Solution

Initial capital investment cost projection is minimal (less than a million dollars) and time to fulfillment less than seven years rather than typically a thirty-year span for large, successful ventures, such as Amazon and Apple.

Review and compare with effective monopolies and their treatment of small business startups discussed in the last paragraph of the first section of this treatise, "How Businesses Are Financed: Then and Now."

The following sets forth how we propose to confront effective monopolies, and invisible forces supporting them, in our business model. All small businesspersons should become aware of the concepts described below. They are the result of a lifetime of experience and attempting to understand what I call "the technology of money," especially as it relates to the political and economic power of the minority diasporas that I want, and need, to protect.

I once attended a conference in San Francisco organized by the UCLA Anderson School of Management, a business school in Los Angeles, California. I received a certificate for my participation over the period of about a week or so. As a small businessman, I clarified many of my ideas and questions about being in business. I also learned a lot of new concepts. I will share the most valuable insight.

How Do You Capture a Market?

There are only three ways. Uniqueness, complementary assets, and speed. The best strategies will attempt to employ all three. But it is difficult to stay unique, it is expensive to accumulate and implement complimentary assets, and the most difficult strategy of all is speed. I then embarked on developing a procedure to use speed effectively. This paper summarizes my conclusions. Now I understand their statement that *speed* was the most difficult but also, when used competently, the most effective.

Speed requires the following:

- coping with the difficulties of maintaining sufficient assets to enable the speed

- the effort necessary to overcome the natural and artificial barriers that result from the constant brilliance and unending perseverance of powerful competitors
- overcoming the effects of simple debilitating fatigue

I approach speed using the ancillary tactics of stealth, deception, and the surprise of superior technology.

The superior technology is that used for building Cal Hacienda homes and includes the on-site manufacture of concrete masonry units, Habiterra Building Technology, and the technology interplay between the five critical elements of twenty-first-century financing.

The five elements to the natural solution are the following:

1. Franchise procedures, *The E-Myth* book strategies. Planned to the point where discretion at the operational level is eliminated.

2. Business credit. As described above, it eliminates the risks of personal guarantees and the new reality of mortgage instability.

3. Internet marketing that requires the four competencies of copywriting, web page design and layout, AdSkills media buying, and customer relations strategies to maintain the integrity of your list of internet clients.

4. Viktor Schauberger's axiom "Comprehend and copy nature" inspired the use of natural strategies. Look at how nature works and how it accomplishes its goals, and follow it. This inspired C. Salazar to develop Virus Tactics Financing, the fastest of all growth strategies. (Viruses go from one unit to millions in just a few hours. Find a way for money to use the same techniques and accomplish the same kind of growth.) Starting with just one unit, grow your capital with the natural speed of virus iterations. Starting with one penny, thirty iterations of each unit separating into two puts you into the millions of dollars.

Direct the building of homes that will, using your proprietary technology, cost $150,000 to build and will sell in today's market for $300,000 to $350,000 each. The sale of each home finances the building of two more. One home's sales proceeds finance the building of two. Two homes finance the building of four, and so on with each home creating two more.

Place the sale proceeds into your IRC Section 1031 tax-free exchange trust. Build and sell 120 homes at $300,000 each, which will total of $36 million. Buy more land and keep going tax-free, or hold the buildings as investments until you need to convert assets to cash.

5. Gunnar Klassen's system that develops many tiny cash flows. He purchased and developed 20,000 buildings with a positive cash flow averaging just $25 each per month. This represents an income of $500,000 a month. He called it his cash flow problem.

If you use virus financing methods described above and organized construction companies that operate like a franchise and have each of them build fifty homes by financing the acquisition, building, and sale using a 1031 tax-free exchange trust and renting out the finished units for a below-market rent that nets $1,000 free and clear income per month. In one or two years, you will have what it took Klassen decades to build. You will have a monthly income of $500,000.

Now watch the interplay between the *twenty-first century's five elements of finance and wealth accumulation.* The interplay can work as follows:

Embark upon a strategy using the Viktor Schauberger-inspired virus financing to organize 1,250 franchise construction companies each building two hundred homes, leave the money in the 1031 exchange trust, and keep the completed four-bedroom, two-bath homes. Then use internet marketing to rent them out for net monthly rental income of $1,000 per home. You will then have a monthly income of $250 million.

Two hundred and fifty million dollars per month is not bad for the interplay of the following:

- franchising procedure
- internet marketing
- virus financing
- maintaining multiple cash flows. $3 billion per year income. Whatever I want to pay taxes on I will keep, and the rest I will donate to my favorite charities who use the money to eliminate

poverty, hunger, human suffering, and afterward provide for universal free education. After taking the charitable and other relevant deductions, I will pay the necessary income taxes.

Or in the unlikely event that I need cash, I can use the income as debt service for $25 billion in leveraged debt where I keep the cash tax-free, but the renters pay off the debt over the term of the loan. I may be liable for income taxes on the small amount of yearly rent that I receive, but I will also have real estate tax losses to offset some or all of it, especially depreciation.

Confronting Global Warming Issues

As part of our development of self-sufficient estates with underground potential, we will use these infrastructure technologies:

- water
- food
- sanitation
- electricity
- communications
- travel
- security

Why Alternative Infrastructure

One reason for developing alternative technology is to acquire land that is inexpensive because it lacks infrastructure. The company can then install our alternative inexpensive infrastructure and build inexpensive homes. Alternative infrastructure gives the company access to inexpensive land for home development. It is here that the company will begin development of self-sufficient homes estates.

A second reason for developing alternative infrastructure is that self-sufficient estates provide a means of survival for families in locations where the government, social, economic, and political framework has failed and is unable to protect and provide for its people. With little warning, this can happen anywhere, anytime, for a variety of reasons, including natural disasters, such as earthquakes, tornadoes, droughts, and hurricanes, electrical grid failures, water system failures, pandemics, and intentional hostile actions, such as strategic commodity (such as oil) embargoes and deliberate acts of war. Today's system of housing development leaves the populace vulnerable to these catastrophes. The ordinary citizen is helpless when these systems fail. The implementation of the self-sufficient protocols means that citizens are no longer helpless.

An integral part of our development of self-sufficient estates with underground potential, we will use these infrastructure technologies in the following ways:

A. Four Water Systems

1. Drill and install a water well going after aquifer or primary water sources.
2. Plan and install a rainwater harvesting system for the one or two times a year that there is substantial rainfall and store it in an underground plastic water tank.
3. Use a dehumidifier to produce water and store in house.
4. Develop and install our brackish or seawater proprietary solar water distillation system using the company's in-house SoVG (Solar-Vacuum-Gravity) system.

B. Sanitation Systems

1. Install septic tank system, gray water system, composting system for soil conditioning, and a biomass digester methane gas generating and storage system.
2. The methane gas is used to fuel the electricity generators that supplement the solar system in charging the batteries that power the electrical system.

C. Agricultural Systems

1. Install Freight Farms mechanized container systems as one source of food production.
2. Install permastructure hothouse agriculture systems as an additional source of food production.
3. Install victory garden growing systems if feasible.
4. Install production system using Fry's Aztec no-waste production structures and his green monster nutrient system.
5. Develop underground systems using LED lighting.
6. Develop a system for cold storage of produce to extend shelf life and earn cash from food producer tenants.
7. Develop a system to market produce to accumulate cash.
8. Develop surpluses that can be marketed and generate cash.

D. Electricity

1. Off-grid solar systems.
2. Battery storage.
3. Electricity generators.
4. Alternative fuels: digester gas, hydrogen electrolyzed from water and other clean sources, and propane if available.

E. Communication.

1. Satellite internet, smartphone, and Television Systems.
2. Ham radio capability.

F. Travel

1. Electric autos.
2. Electric bicycles and wagons.
3. Electric motor gliders aircraft.
4. Hydrogen-converted engines.

G. Security: Hire Professional Services

Practical Approach to Global Warming Survival

To cope with issues that may arise from global warming, at some point, we will start constructing communities that are partially underground. We will use earthmovers to remove twenty to thirty feet of soil. We will build the very inexpensive Cal Earth type dome structures and develop practical infrastructure to service them. Out desert communities will have structures both above and below ground. In periods of extreme weather, the self-sufficient, sustainable, and underground shelters should provide a comfortable refuge.

Economic Vehicles for Dual Participation with the Larger Economy

Although we expect to first confront the affordability issue in housing, we also intend to develop self-sufficient, sustainable communities. These communities can sustain themselves without interacting with the larger economy. However, for those who wish to do so, vehicles will be developed to enable interaction with the larger economy. We will sell surplus food to farmer's markets, produce brokers, restaurants, supermarket chains, and any other markets that are profitable. We will also provide communications technology so that internet businesses are available through our communities. We will sponsor scholarships to young people to go away to college and enter the greater economy but always have the option to come home and be welcomed. There will always be a meaningful place for our returning young people and their families.

Urban and Rural Housing Production

As we approach affordable housing production, we will focus on affordability, self-sufficient sustainability, and access for both rural and urban communities. There are challenges in design for urban areas that we are working on. Indoor food production and underground gardens are feasible. We intend to confront the financial barriers in rural areas to also increase affordability, even for the very poor, along with self-sufficient sustainability and access to all income levels.

Leverage Theory versus Lessons of Nature Theory

How Leverage Works to Achieve Rapid Growth

Leverage is well understood in modern finance as a tool used to speed financial growth. In Greek mythology, Atlas is supposed to have boasted that if he had a lever that was long enough, he could lift the world. In finance, the idea is to use a small amount of money to move a large amount and make your profit on the large number. To illustrate how it works, assume that you had $10,000 to invest and assume you had an opportunity to earn interest of 10 percent per year. If you invested, a year later your $10,000 would have earned you an increase in wealth of $1,000 in interest income. But if you used the $10,000 as a down payment to leverage a $90,000 loan to purchase a $100,000 parcel of property and the property increased in value 10 percent. You could then sell the property for $110,000 and be left with $20,000 after paying off your $90,000 loan. Now your $10,000 has earned you a profit of $10,000 or 100 percent on your investment of $10,000. Without leverage, you earned $1,000. With leverage, you earned $10,000. The downside to leverage is that if the property loses 10 percent in value and you have to sell it for $90,000 to pay off the loan, your investment is a total loss. You can be wiped out quickly when leverage works against you. Leverage is a gamble whereby you can lose just as much as you can win. I have heard bankers discussing not lending to clients who they believed were overleveraged.

To use leverage, an entrepreneur must have a lender, generally arranged by a banker, to lend the leveraged funds. Remember the banker's golden rule. He who has the gold makes the rules. In the negotiations for loans, the bankers will insist on transferring most of the risk to the borrower as a condition for making the loan.

Interest payments, financial statements, and taxes are all computed on the basis of yearly rates of profit or loss. Scorekeeping computed on an annual basis is the name of the game.

Leverage is a widely understood concept in finance and used extensively in real estate. Homeownership, the basis of middle-class wealth accumulation, is based on leverage. A small down payment enables bankers to lend a huge mortgage amount. Middle-class wealth could not have been created without the mortgage loans that fueled the industry.

How "Lessons of Nature" Works to Achieve Rapid Growth

Viktor Schauberger, a Bavarian forest official in the 1930s, preached to comprehend and copy nature. That led me to look for natural methods of achieving rapid growth. I hit upon infections. Just one cell of a virus can infect an organism, and within a few days, millions of cells will have grown within the organism in an out-of-control infection. I thought, *What if you could grow money as fast as a virus? Can I copy what nature does? How does nature do it? It depends on the qualities of the virus cell. Can it reproduce itself?* If you can create a product that enable the creation of two more and each of them do likewise, you, like a virus growing, can achieve exponential progression. Linear progression grows per iteration like this: one, two, three, four, etc. Whereas exponential progression grows per iteration like this: two, four, eight, sixteen, thirty-two, etc. Starting with a penny, by the thirtieth iteration, you are over a million dollars. There are few business opportunities that can provide a product that can do this, mostly because no one believes that exponential progress is practical even if it were possible. I believe I have recognized a unique situation where I can use virus financing tactics to accomplish exponential growth.

History will tell whether I am right and whether I can use it as a force for good in the world.

Comparative Risk Analysis between Leverage and Virus Tactics

- Leverage risks: The risk of leverage is not being able to make the payments because of losses due to vacancies, loss of employment, and/or other catastrophes that diminish cash flow. This is when bankers switch from pretending to be your friends to your economic predators. They are so sorry to be forced to foreclose on your home and put you, and your family, out on the street. They are then the new owners of your property.
- Lenders' transfer of risk.
- Costs of points and interest.
- Market risk that property can't be sold or rented.
- Excessive leverage losses as opposed to normal losses.
- Scorekeeping is based on annual rates for computation of interest rates and financial statements.

Virus Tactics Risks and Rewards

The feasibility study and assumptions may be incorrect, and the initial investment may not be sufficient to complete and sell the initial projects built using virus tactics.

Market risk during complete plowback of funds into business during initial iterations.

Once underway, when each home is completed, it has been paid for by the sale of the previous home and is owned free and clear. There are real risks at the beginning, but then they disappear.

With leverage, as the projects grow and get bigger, the risks also increase and the chances that you will be caught in a recession or some type of downturn and lose everything constantly increases.

The value of virus tactics is that there is a relatively small risk at the beginning, but then the risks disappear and the rewards are not only enormous but astronomical.

Real Estate Wealth Forces in Twenty-First-Century America

Some prominent vendors of real estate advice state the following: align your interest with the following forces, and your wealth will increase as time passes.

Force	Our System's Performance
• Inflation	Real estate value rises with inflation.
• Interest Rates	We self-finance our construction. The interest stays at home.
• Taxes	We operate through IRC Section 1031 tax-free exchange trusts. No taxes until we withdraw cash. We will donate to 501(c)(3) nonprofit corporations, take the charitable deductions, and plan every legal tax avoidance action possible.
• Opportunity Costs Disappear	We self-finance. Any interest stays home. We engage in tax-free exchanges with gains measured in terms of monthly iterations rather than annual calculations. This is the opportunity with the highest yield. This system grows faster than leveraged systems and is immune to the risks of leverage.

PART 3

IT'S TIME TO MAKE LUCK HAPPEN FOR THE LEFT BEHIND

Rather than simply observing that the divide between the rich and the poor is rapidly accelerating, it is more precise to say that the American middle class is now divided between those who own homes in nice neighborhoods, and therefore the *soon to be rich,* and those who are being *left behind* because they cannot afford a home.

Economics trends tend to begin in California and migrate eastward and develop throughout the nation. What is true today for Southern California may soon be true in most of the nation. Today's potential home buyers in Southern California are divided between the 25 percent who have the financial capability to purchase a home and the 75 percent who have been priced out of the market. Since home prices tend to rise faster than wages, today's economy is much more volatile than at the time of secure union, and otherwise comparably stable, jobs of the 1950s and 1960s. Once home prices exceed a buyer's income capability, it becomes very difficult to catch up, and most are left behind. Homeownership and the benefits it brings to a family's prospects become a distant dream that fades as the middle class continues to evaporate.

The Opportunity Presented by the 2023 Housing Market in California: A Proving Ground Opportunity for Virus Tactics

In today's market where the median price of a new home is about $800,000 and median income is about $56,000, 75 percent of the market cannot qualify for the mortgage loans necessary, especially while paying rapidly rising interest rates. Current trends indicate that those most in need cannot and, going forward, will be unable to purchase a home.

In these circumstances, it appears possible to use virus tactics. This is because leaders are aware that they must develop a way where each home sale can generate sufficient funds to completely finance the construction of two more without bankers and the growth can be tax-free through an IRC Section 1031 tax-free exchanges. Build and hold, sell and trade, find and buy building sites, and repeat as often as possible. Build and sell through eight or ten iterations, and you can generate adequate capital to begin to make a difference.

Are the "Lessons of Nature Virus Tactics" feasible as a practical method of financing businesses and development projects? Business theorists contemplate that a 10 percent to 20 percent profit per year is a healthy margin. Competition should regulate the market to keep profits in this range. There are probably some businesses where a 4 percent profit looks good. Virus tactics would require a profit of 100 percent per iteration, not per year. If you have five iterations in a year, it will equate to a 500 percent profit per year. How can this be considered feasible? If it were that easy, everyone would use it. This can't be practical.

The Need to Identify and Recognize Virus Tactics Opportunities

When I first learned how to develop larger office buildings and apartment projects, I had to do feasibility studies. Most are not feasible. You must develop a sense for what may be possible, then you need to conduct feasibility research and analysis. The projects that do get built are not those that are feasible—there are almost none that are feasible at first blush—but those where the developer's creativity and skills for innovation find a way to make the project become feasible. It doesn't just work, but only works after a lot of work, innovation, and sometimes just a lucky break.

As is the case with any development project, you must search for the appropriate opportunity where you can arrange assets and opportunities into a plan where virus tactics can work. I believe I have found one by modifying a new building technology that allows me to cut building costs at a time when housing prices are at an all-time high. Because of my work with Schauberger's lessons of nature and my experience as a real estate developer, I was able to recognize the opportunity and was experienced enough to make a serious attempt to seize it. Like all real estate development projects, you must be lucky. Specifically, the luck you get when you are sufficiently prepared to recognize opportunities and are sufficiently prepared to seize the opportunity. To successfully exploit virus tactics, you must search for, and identify, the opportunities where it will work. In this way, it is like any other development project.

Being a leader who believes that he can make a difference in this situation, I have a duty to try. I have found that when it comes to aiding the poor, the weak, and the unfortunate, if there is no immediate payment or substantial profit, persons who are trained and competent generally do not want to be bothered. Most of those who truly care and want to help do not have the skills, training, and capital to make a difference. Those who can, won't, and those who will, can't. A poverty warrior learns empowering skills so that he both can and will make a difference.

The plan is to develop profitable housing developments and recruit and train economic casualties of the current housing market as construction workers who can thusly qualify as partners in future developments where eventually their distribution would be a home that they helped construct. The basic design would be concrete block, 1,200-square-foot, four-bedroom, two-bath homes and sell and trade them in a manner that returns double the capital back to the developers. This allows the next development to be twice the size of the previous one. It will not take long to start making a difference. As poor, weak, and unfortunate persons start to acquire homes free and clear of mortgage loans, word will spread, making recruiting a simple matter. The goal is to build at least 250,000 affordable homes while perfecting the techniques of self-sufficiency and the development of self-sufficient estates.

The most difficult part was to develop the initial projects without seeking support of financial partners and investment bankers. These require exorbitant profit and demand control. If successful, they squeeze out as much profit as possible and squeeze out the partners. Whereas the originators may follow the Christian golden rule of doing unto others as you would have them do unto you, the financial partners historically follow the banker's golden rule that he who has the gold makes the rules. Moreover, frequently they engage in the business golden rule of doing unto others as they would do to you, but do it first. Historically, this has always meant that the poor, weak, and unfortunates will be outmaneuvered and left behind. Therefore, to be successful in making luck happen for the left behind, the program must be bootstrapped into existence and develop growth capital from internal operations.

This may appear to be a daunting task, but it is not unusual for problem-solvers, like my wife, who have learned that *there is always a way.* A major tenant of lesson 6 of the book *Make Luck Happen* states, "If your heart is big enough, you plan, based on experience, smart enough, and your perseverance tough enough, then you can successfully confront any problem or adversary no matter how big or powerful."

An entity has been formed, Cal Hacienda Inc., and a plan has been developed and is being implemented. Bootstrapping is slow developing but provides time to do detailed research and planning that enhances prospects for success.

Once the program is underway and a success, then we can start focusing on the challenges presented by global warming for Cal Hacienda communities. We will build our standard homes aboveground and dig out desert land and start building dome outbuildings, then replace the soil so that these dome homes and ancillary buildings are underground. They will use light and water to grow food underground, leave batteries and solar infrastructure underground, and leave or build additional underground buildings. All equipment except solar panels will remain underground for protection. Surplus food will be sold to kick-start an underground economy. We will install satellite communications and engage in the internet economy. We will use newly acquired home building skills to license our companies as a B-1 building contractor and build homes for the market economy. We will learn skills to teach useful capabilities to build the alternative underground economy. Long-term survival from attacks by competitors and the risk of entrepreneurship require that we comply scrupulously to pay legitimate taxes and stay legal in our operations to avoid oppression.

Observations and Questions

(Leading to the Creation of This Book)

Do middle-class Americans recognize their peril?

- Although disasters appear to be natural, the causes of their severity are man-made.
- Despite warnings, Americans continue to die in their homes today, destroyed by the new intensity of wildfires, hurricanes, and floods.

It is only the beginning. The peril is constant. This book proposes pathways to avoid these perils. But how was it even possible to destabilize America's wealthy middle class? Note the following tactics:

1. Subdue the middle-class student protest battle force with debt. (It's called *peonage*—from GI bill *grants* to predatory student *loans* that limit bankruptcy.)
2. Destroy major sources of wage income through automation and globalization.
3. Harness bankers' greed by engaging in massive fraudulent abuse of mortgage-backed securities to destroy even the notion of new homeownership for many. This eliminates the primary source of new wealth for the middle and rising working classes. (See the film *The Big Short* that exposes the fraud: affordable home building atrophied for thirteen years and can't quickly recover due to the antihousing NIMBY political movements, credit tightening, and expensive construction.)

Are these the result of intentional attacks on the middle class, or are they only a coincidence?

This book describes how finance really works. Finance and land have been used as hostile weapons in the past.

Options are recommended for using education and training, human sweat, homegrown commodities, alternate financing tactics, and land to successfully manage and avoid current foreseeable misfortunes aimed at middle-class disruption and disaster.

These options enable renewed sources of wealth creation to stimulate middle-class growth.

Leadership is needed to implement solutions to the foreseeable challenges to middle-class survival.

Addendum

After completing the draft manuscript of this book, I encountered Noam Chomsky's *Requiem for the American Dream*. It paralleled my inquiry from a different focus and sought solutions from a different time. He saw hope for the American dream through participatory democracy and observed that the primary force that has consistently stood in opposition to concentrations of wealth and power has been organized labor. He further observed that the labor movement tactics of street protests of the 1930s were effective and noted their similarity with the events surrounding the street protests of the civil rights and anti-Vietnam War movements. He seemed to infer that, in his experience, the most effective tactic against wealth and power was embodied in street protest.

On the other hand, the path advocated in this book follows a purely middle-class strategy to defending democracy and furthering the interest of the middle class. Below, I summarize the differences.

Noam Chomsky's *Requiem for the American Dream: Ten Principles of Concentration of Wealth and Power*

The vile cycle that creates and continually increases inequality works as follows: Wealth brings political power that the wealthy uses to protect their interest, no matter how detrimental or harmful to others. The wealthy use their power to increase their wealth, which leads to more power. The cycle continues as the rich get richer and the less wealthy get left behind and the distance between the rich and the lower classes enlarges.

Adam Smith's book *The Wealth of Nations* described the upper class. "All for ourselves and nothing for other people seems, in every age of the world, to have been the vile maxim of the Master of Mankind."

Principle 1: Reduce Democracy

Democracy's age-old problem is to deter the more numerous poor from voting to take everything from the wealthy. There are two solutions.

Madison said to reduce democracy.

Aristotle said to reduce inequality.

This book's solution reduces inequality.

Principle 2: Shape Ideology

Principle 3: Redesign the Economy

Shift power to financial institutions, the money brokers (the bankers). Go from wealth producers to money manipulators.

Principle 4: Shift the Burden

Shift the burden away from the wealthy to the *precariat* (precarious proletariat, maintained by job insecurity), who pay taxes rather than use loopholes to avoid them.

Wealth in 1950: 38 percent producers and 11 percent bankers. During period of regulation, there were no crashes.

In 2022 after deregulation, over 90 percent of wealth held by bankers; crashes stemming from greed are now almost predictable.

Globalization put workers around the world in competition with each other.

Principle 5: Attack Solidarity (or Its Symptoms Like Social Security and Public Schools)

Principle 6: Run the Regulators

Regulatory capture.

Principle 7: Engineer Elections

The costs of elections send politicians into the hands of the rich.

Principle 8: Keep the Rabble in Line

Labor unions now only represent 7 percent of private business. The engine for change is generally found in the streets. Chomsky saw the bodies in the streets during the labor movement of the 1930s, the civil rights movement, and more particularly, the protests against the war in Vietnam in the late 1960s and early 1970s. These were the most effective engines for change in his lifetime. (I have observed that the countermove that has been successfully used to keep these rabble in line has not been jail—jail has never worked—but student debt implemented as a form of peonage.)

Principle 9: Manufacture Consent

Consumers are directed to the superficial away from serious confrontations.

Principle 10: Marginalize the Population

Never allow them a vehicle that seriously influences policy. Seventy percent of the population feels powerless and unable to influence policy. They are full of anger and unstructured hate. Propaganda teaches them to hate and fear each other. Elections can be manipulated, and both sides are already beholden to the wealthy and powerful.

Different Approaches

Chomsky's the streets and revolution versus Rico Vidas's trained, experienced leadership using the protocols of problem-solving with the results evaluated according to principles of American pragmatism.

American pragmatism promotes the following:

- the quality of being fit or suitable to bring about a desired end
- the ability to make considered decisions or come to sensible conclusions

These qualities are the goal for participants in the Cal Hacienda programs.

Pragmatism is the school of philosophy that was dominant in the United States in the first quarter of the twentieth century. *It is based on the principle that the usefulness, workability, and practicality of ideas, policies, and proposals are the criteria of their merit.*

It values the pursuit of practicality over aesthetic qualities.

The first Rico Vidas treatise, *Make Luck Happen,* promotes learning substantive leadership through utilization of the protocols of problem-solving practice and experience. Practice and experience empower these leaders to make things happen. "If your heart is big enough, your plan, based on experience, smart enough, and your perseverance tough enough, then you can successfully confront any problem or adversary, no matter how difficult and/or powerful."

Lack of sufficient finances is simply part of the problem that must be included in its definition. A strategy to overcome this and other barriers must be formulated and implemented. Follow the protocols of problem-solving to develop and carry out your plan.

If you reach a point where you feel unable to come up with or create a suitable strategy, inquire and research how other leaders throughout history have successfully confronted these kinds of problems. Almost any problem that you may encounter has been successfully confronted by someone in the past.

Examine and evaluate this approach to building affordable housing to perpetuate the middle class using the tools I have outlined in this treatise and in *Make Luck Happen*.

Rather than resorting to the streets or a violent revolution, a competent leader, trained in our system, will bring about a superior result in less time with far less suffering. But importantly, he or she will not be obligated or indebted to bankers or others whose interest is different from our own middle class.